# Olde

# COTSWOLD
# PUNISHMENTS

# Olde
# COTSWOLD
# PUNISHMENTS

*Nell Darby*

The
History
Press

First published 2011

The History Press
The Mill, Brimscombe Port
Stroud, Gloucestershire, GL5 2QG
www.thehistorypress.co.uk

British Library Cataloguing in Publication Data.
A catalogue record for this book is available from the British Library.

ISBN 978 0 7524 5815 1

Typesetting and origination by The History Press
Printed in Great Britain

# CONTENTS

# ACKNOWLEDGEMENTS

I would like to thank the staff of the Gloucestershire Archives and National Archives for their help in obtaining records for me – in some cases they were very musty eighteenth-century archives that looked as though they hadn't been accessed in quite some time!

I would also like to thank my family – John, Jake and Eva Darby – for their encouragement and support throughout the research and writing process.

# INTRODUCTION

Crime and punishment have both fascinated and repelled us for centuries, but in an age and society where the usual punishment for crimes consists of community service, Anti-Social Behaviour Orders (ASBO), or prison sentences regarded by the right-wing media as little different to short stays in hotels, the punishments of the past seem both different and more imaginative.

Until the middle of the eighteenth century, many common law crimes were punishable by hanging, and although statutes were brought in from then on that limited the use of the death penalty, there were still, to our eyes, a multitude of crimes that could be punished by death. In fact, the Bloody Code of the eighteenth century enabled courts to sentence to death those guilty of minor property crimes, such as thefts, that to us seem very petty. Hanging was usual, but burning at the stake, being hanged in chains, or being drawn and quartered were also accepted forms of punishment practiced well into the eighteenth century. Suicides fared little better; if someone was deemed to have been sane when they killed themselves, regardless of the reasons for their decision, they would be buried in unconsecrated ground. One Gloucestershire man, Samuel Cooper, who had hanged himself from a bacon rack at his house in the Forest of Dean in 1752, was buried at a crossroads outside his town, with a stake driven through his body.[1]

And those punishments that allowed criminals to stay alive seem little better than the death penalty. Many men and women were ordered to be transported to America, and, after the Civil War, to Australia – countries far, far away from their homes, families and friends, where they risked dying on the voyage out, and might have to stay for life.

Punishments for petty crimes seem, to modern eyes, arbitrary and overly severe in many cases, with some punishments designed to humiliate the criminal in front of his neighbours – most parishes, towns and counties had their own pillories, stocks, or whipping posts. Some punishments were targeted at women who transgressed the unwritten rules of society, with ducking ponds and scolds' bridles designed to embarrass and quieten women seen as being scolds to their husbands or generally troublesome.

The people of the Cotswolds, although fascinated by tales of crime, seemed to find the punishments meted out in other areas more interesting than those in their own region – perhaps in the belief that they were a more civilised region, and so could read about crimes in other areas as though not affecting them. The *Gloucester Journal* throughout the eighteenth century contained many stories of miscreants being punished in London and the south-east, as well as promotions for execution ballads and pamphlets, yet rarely covered convictions in Gloucestershire. There was the odd mention of the assizes, but it was usually to detail those people who would be tried, rather than covering their trials or convictions.

In August 1730, for example, the *Gloucester Journal* featured convictions at the assizes in Kingston, Surrey, eagerly reporting that 'one was burnt in the Hand for manslaughter, several Order'd for Transportation, and four to be whipt.'[2] Perhaps the branding of the hand was rare enough in England to merit a mention in this local paper, although there were plenty of whipping and transportation sentences in Gloucestershire without mentioning those in Surrey.

However, the *Gloucester Journal* saw its role as covering national and international events, enabling literate Gloucestershire folk to learn about the wider world and feel quite cosmopolitan. Local events, which would have made the paper appear too provincial, were reduced to a few lines, so given far less prominence than the many adverts for products and shops in the area.

This skewing of coverage of the assizes has the effect of making it look as though the Cotswolds, and Gloucestershire as a whole, were more

law-abiding than other parts of England, but this
wasn't the case; there were plenty of local trials,
as the brief mentions in the *Gloucester Journal*'s
inquest and court coverage show. The patterns
in cases, and the punishments meted out to the
convicted, demonstrate the changes in methods of
punishment in the area over time. Through a study
of cases heard at the Gloucestershire Assizes, a lot
can be learned about attitudes towards crime and
punishment both in the area and at a national level,
and how they gradually changed over time.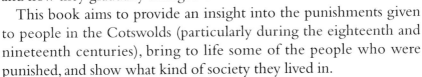

This book aims to provide an insight into the punishments given
to people in the Cotswolds (particularly during the eighteenth and
nineteenth centuries), bring to life some of the people who were
punished, and show what kind of society they lived in.

*Nell Darby, 2011*

## Notes

[1] *Gloucester Journal*, 31 March 1752
[2] *Gloucester Journal*, 11 August 1730

# 1

# BURNED AT THE STAKE

From our viewpoint, in the twenty-first century, we might view capital punishment of any kind with abhorrence, looking at the hangings of the past as a sign of an uncivilised British society - although some people would still prefer it if we had capital punishment. Yet up to the mid-eighteenth century, some crimes were deemed to be such an affront to the natural condition of society that they deserved to be punished with a death worse than hanging. Hanging, after all, could – if you were lucky – result in a quick death from a dislocated or broken neck; even if you were unlucky, strangulation from the rope might only take minutes.

So for crimes regarded as being petty treason – such as a woman murdering her husband, viewed as an unnatural state of affairs, for the wife should be subservient to her spouse – a different form of death was used. The guilty would be burned to death.

This sentence was also used in Britain as a punishment for heretics, those seen to be against the established order, and the Cotswolds had a long association with the punishment. In the sixteenth century, the Bishop of Gloucester, John Hooper, was martyred by being burned at the stake. Possibly raised in Oxfordshire, he had graduated from Oxford University in 1519 and after a varied career, became Bishop of Gloucester in 1550. A Protestant reformer, he caused controversy by rejecting the wearing of clerical vestments in the Church of England, thus violating the 1549 Act

Oxford, where John Hooper studied.

of Uniformity. His radical views made him a marked man. He was initially imprisoned on the charge of owing the Crown money and was deprived of his bishopric. He was eventually executed at Gloucester on 9 February 1555, his death a drawn-out affair due to the faggots placed at the stake being made of green wood, and taking time to catch fire.[1]

Within 200 years the punishment was being meted out to those guilty of less cerebral or religious crimes – domestic crimes committed by women, seen as more of an affront to society than those committed by men, were singled out for such a sentence.

For example, in March 1723, Jane Leamoucks, of Gloucester, was indicted for the murder of her husband James. It was alleged that she had stabbed him in the stomach with a knife on 12 October 1722. Several witnesses were called to give evidence at her trial, and said that they had often heard her threatening to kill James; another witness, John Harding, said further that she had admitted stabbing her husband and had asked Harding to hide the knife in her garden so that it wouldn't be found. The court heard that she was a 'person of a very bad character' and found her guilty of wilful murder.

On 1 April 1723, she was burned to death, probably near to her own house, at the scene of the crime. The *Gloucester Journal* reported that she denied committing the murder right up to her death, and 'behaved herself very stubborn, from the time of her receiving sentence to the place of execution'.[2]

Thirty years later, on 14 April 1753, Ann Williams was burnt at the stake for poisoning her husband.[3] The Newgate Calendar described her as being a 'turbulent and dictatorial' woman who ruled over her mild-mannered husband 'with a rod of iron'.[4] Mr Williams had grown used to letting his wife have her own way, and his subservient attitude caused her to regard him with contempt and dislike. Ann, subsumed by dislike for the man she was bound to in law, and cheating on him with another man, got her servant to buy some white mercury, and poisoned both her husband's gruel and ale. He underwent a horrible death, in pain and constantly vomiting, accusing his wife on his deathbed of murdering him and calling Ann a 'wicked woman'.

Given the nature of Mr Williams' death, and the evidence for the purchase of the poison, Ann was found guilty of her husband's murder and sentenced to death. Even up to the point that she was burnt, though – the sentence being carried out on 13 April 1753 - she continued to deny being responsible.[5]

Ann's burning would have been carried out at Over, a small village just outside Gloucester. This was where the county's gallows stood, until they were relocated to Gloucester Prison. She may have been taken from the prison to Over on a hurdle, before being chained to a wooden stake, around which would be heaped faggots. Although the sight of a woman burning to death sounds appalling to modern ears, Ann Williams' punishment was witnessed by a crowd of onlookers. The only consolation for the squeamish is that many women were in fact strangled with a rope before being tied to the stake, out of a strange kind of sympathy for their sufferings, meaning that they were, in effect, hanged before being burned.

Burning continued to be the sentence for women convicted either of petty treason or high treason, which included coining offences. The last death by burning in Britain was, according to Richard Clark, in 1789,[6] while Ann Williams' was the last recorded case in Gloucestershire.

Subsequently, women convicted of killing their husbands were hanged for their crimes. Their offences may still have been seen as being unnatural acts for a woman to commit, but they were now punished in the same way as men. So Harriet Tarver, the young woman from Chipping Campden who was hanged on 9 April 1836 after poisoning her husband, had a far quicker death than Ann Williams – although she possibly had more lasting notoriety,

Harriet Tarver poisoned her husband in Chipping Campden.

a broadsheet ballad being composed and sold to mark the occasion of her execution.[7]

## Notes

[1] 'John Hooper, Bishop of Gloucester and Worcester and Protestant Martyr' from the *Oxford Dictionary of National Biography*, accessed at http://www.oxforddnb.com/view/article/13706

[2] *Gloucester Journal*, 1 April 1723, accessed via http://genebug.net/glsinquests.htm.

[3] *Gloucester Journal*, 17 April 1753, via http://genebug.net/glsinquests.htm

[4] The Newgate Calendar, accessed via http://www.exclassics.com/newgate/ng432.htm

[5] The Newgate Calendar, http://www.exclassics.com/newgate/ng432.htm

[6] Capital Punishment UK, accessed via http://www.capitalpunishmentuk.org/burning.htm

[7] Nell Darby (2009) pp 118-125

# 2

# HANGED IN CHAINS

Hanging, as the ultimate punishment for criminals, has existed in England since Anglo-Saxon times, and wasn't outlawed until 1964. Within this broad expanse of time, methods of hanging have changed; additional humiliations have been added to the punishment, such as hanging in chains or in a cage, being drawn and quartered afterwards, or bodies being left on show to the public until they rotted; but the mode of death has remained the same.

People from all classes have been hanged; when the authorities wanted to make a public example of those deemed to have committed extraordinarily bad crimes, they would give them the additional punishment of being hanged in chains, known as gibbeting. One notorious case in the Cotswolds came in 1549, when vicar Henry Joyce was hanged in chains from the tower of his church, St Mary's in Chipping Norton, as a punishment for taking part in the Oxfordshire Rising, a protest against the introduction of the New English Prayer Book.[1]

Our nineteenth-century ancestors were famously fascinated and repelled in equal measure when it came to public executions. Crowds would gather in advance of the hangings of notorious criminals, with entrepreneurial landowners close to scaffold sites erecting seats for spectators, memorabilia being produced and sold, broadsheet ballads purporting to represent the chain of events, and the criminal's final words being composed and sold before the said criminal had had the chance to utter any such final words.

St Mary's Church, Chipping
Norton, where a former vicar
was hung in chains.

Charles Dickens attended executions and was left repelled by the public reaction; but the disquiet he felt was not shared by the majority of those attending an execution for a day out.

Public hangings were eventually replaced by private affairs that took place within the confines of the prison walls in 1868, ending a centuries-old tradition of public humiliation. The last public hanging in Gloucestershire took place four years earlier, in 1864, when Lewis Gough was hanged at Gloucester Prison for murdering Mary Curtis;[2] the first private hanging there wasn't until 1872, when Frederick Jones, aged twenty, was hanged for killing his girlfriend, Emily Gardner in Cheltenham.[3]

But the public execution of criminals had another purpose aside from making the criminal recognise the enormity of his or her crime. It was intended that members of the public watching someone else undergo an awful death would be deterred from committing crimes themselves, aware of what fate might befall them if they did. Whether it had this effect is debatable, but the public certainly attended executions in great numbers. Gibbeting was also intended to deter others – by hanging criminals in public places and leaving their bodies to rot in front of passers-by.

When a simple man named Eli Hatton was sentenced to hang in chains in Mitcheldean, at the other end of Gloucestershire, on 4 September 1732, after smashing the head of a widowed carpenter with an axe, some 10,000 people were estimated to have watched his execution. He was pushed off a ladder whilst tied to a tree at Meane Hill, near Mitcheldean, and while denying the murder to the end, confessed to being a 'great Sabbath breaker' and being 'addicted to whoring'. This was, though, according to the local paper's report, which printed a full and detailed account of his death, whilst mentioning that he needed to confess his varied other sins because they 'gave his conscience the greatest uneasiness'.[4] One wonders whether the illiterate man said all this as he was about to die, or whether the newspaper was attempting to meet a public service remit by warning its readers of the dangers of breaking the Sabbath. Its account of Eli Hatton's death was reminiscent of the broadsheet ballads published after executions, which stressed the importance of morality whilst going into salacious detail about criminal acts.

Another case where the Cotswold public flocked to see justice done – or just to watch men shudder in the hangman's noose, depending on your point of view – was the hanging of Thomas Cambrey on 24 March 1744 at Bowling Green, Cirencester. I have written more fully about the case elsewhere,[5] but Cambrey, who had been convicted of murdering Anne Millington after a house robbery went wrong, was hanged in chains near the Millington house, and the *Gloucester Journal* reported that 'there was the greatest number of people ever seen on such an occasion', which also saw spectators attempting to argue with the condemned man about what he had or hadn't done.[6]

The Stow-on-the-Wold petty sessions, usually held at the Unicorn Inn, attracted the attention of local residents keen to hear what had been going on, who was involved, and how they would be punished. According to Joan Johnson, in her history of the town, when cases were referred from the Justice of the Peace at the petty sessions to the county assizes at Gloucester, 'crowds of people' would walk from Stow to Gloucester to wait for convictions and watch the executions that might subsequently take place. Walking nearly 30 miles to see an execution, and then walking the same distance back, sounds more like a big excursion for some entertainment than a desire to learn from others' mistakes.[7]

The Unicorn Hotel – formerly Inn – in Stow-on-the-Wold.

Up until the early nineteenth century, one of the main ways in which society punished murderers was by hanging these criminals in chains, on a gibbet, often erected close to the scene of their crime, or close to major roads or crossroads, both to link their crime with their death, and to show their fate to the maximum number of passers-by. Eli Hatton's body, for example, was left hanging on the gibbet for two months after his execution, and, after the gibbet was finally removed in November 1732, the murderer's body was left in a heap on the ground, unburied.[8] On Durdham Down, Bristol, the bodies of two other murderers who had been hanged in chains – Henry Payne and Andrew Burnet – were stolen off the gibbet in late April 1744, a month after they had been executed. Their bodies were later found hidden amongst rocks on the downs – and they were promptly hung up again.[9]

To be hanged in chains had originally been a punishment under common law, and judges could impose the penalty in addition to the usual sentence of execution. In 1751, the sentence was formalised in law when the Murder Act was passed. The Murder Act, which came into effect in 1752, enabled judges to set gibbeting as a punishment for murder. This Act stated that the bodies of murderers shouldn't be buried, but should either be dissected or left hanging in chains. It also stipulated that this public punishment was intended to add 'some further terror and peculiar mark of infamy' to the punishment of being hanged, and thereby prevent others from committing murder.[10]

The punishment was often imposed not only for murder but also for committing highway robbery and sheep stealing – both common crimes in the rural Cotswolds, with their multiplicity of valuable animals and dark, dangerous country lanes. One of the most infamous of seventeenth-century highwaymen, James Hind, was from the Chipping Norton area of the Oxfordshire Cotswolds – he ended up being hung, drawn and quartered for treason at Worcester in 1652, his head and body parts afterwards being displayed on gates around the town.[11]

In the late eighteenth century, the Dunsdon brothers, who were sibling highwaymen, roamed the Oxfordshire side of the Cotswolds. They were named Tom, Dick and Harry, which is where we get the popular saying (it could be any old Tom, Dick or Harry).

Fulbrook, home of the Dunsdon brothers.

From Fulbrook, near Burford, they were known as the Burford Highwaymen,[12] although they were also common burglars, robbing farmers and local houseowners of livestock, money and possessions. The Wychwood Forest – then much larger than now – was their preferred hiding place for their loot. They progressed to robbing coaches, including, so legend has it, the Gloucester to Oxford coach.

When the brothers committed one robbery at Tangley Hall, just outside Burford, the owner was tipped-off and managed to tie Dick Dunsdon's arm to a door bolt, making it impossible for him to escape. One of his brothers then cut off the lower part of his arm with his sword to enable him to flee, but he is believed to have bled to death shortly afterwards.

Tom and Harry continued to live in the local area, but were captured after attending the Burford Whitsuntide Festival, which was held at Capps Lodge, between Burford and Shipton upon Cherwell. Although the locals knew who they were, they were in such fear of the brothers that they didn't try to stop them attending. The Dunsdons played card games with local festival goers until four o'clock the next morning, and after losing a game, fought with tapster William Harding, whom Harry then shot in the arm and chest. A local ostler named Perkins managed to grab Tom Dunsdon's pistol and hit

A view over Capps Lodge.

him on the head, knocking him out. A fight broke out between the others present, before Harry again fired at Harding.

A policeman was called from nearby Widford. PC Secker, with the help of others, managed to capture the brothers and transport them to Gloucester Gaol. When Harding died a couple of weeks later, the brothers were charged with murder. The judge described the Dunsdons as 'desperate fellows who had long been a terror to the country where they lived' and sentenced them to be hung in chains. They were hanged from a gibbet constructed on a tree on the edge of the Wychwood Forest in 1784.[13]

As a footnote, the local Wychwood Brewery claims that on an oak tree near the Farmer Inn, at Capps Lodge, the initials 'H.D., T.D.' are inscribed into the bark.[14] If these are, as legend has it, the initials of two of the Dunsdon brothers, it would be a nice link to the area, but it may well be just a rural, as opposed to urban, legend.

The Dunsdon brothers went down in history as romantic highwaymen, both feared and revered by a local population who saw them as rebelling against convention and the law. But common murderers were not seen in so rosy a light, and their deaths were viewed as fully justified, before being promptly forgotten.

In 1727, Roger Bryant was condemned to be hanged in chains on Tug Hill, in the west of Gloucestershire, after being convicted of murdering a lady called Anne Williams. The Gloucester Assizes heard that on 3 April in

that year, he had broken into the house of Tobias Luton at Tug Hill, Doynton, to steal a number of silver and gold items. He was surprised by the Luton family's servant – Anne Williams – and hit her over the head, killing her.

Roger was twenty-four and from a poor Doynton family – he was described as being 'born of mean Parentage'. He was originally a sheerman's apprentice, but disliked the work and ran away from his employer – a criminal offence in itself. He then joined the army, but deserted. He was described in court as 'a person of ill-repute' who tried to blame another man, John Evans, for the murder. This was despite the fact that Bryant was identified as having sold one of Luton's rings at Cirencester, and had correctly pinpointed where other Luton belongings were hidden. John Evans was duly reprieved, but Bryant was hanged in chains on 12 August 1727 on Tug Hill, close to the Luton family home.[15]

On 14 March 1763, a Wyck Rissington man was found guilty of murder and sentenced to be hanged in chains. Thomas Hanks' trial lasted seven hours, during which the jury heard that he had murdered his wife, Ann. Despite his protestations of innocence, everybody in court, apparently, was concerned about Hanks' 'obdurate insensibility' of the gravity of the charge against him. His mother, who had been charged as being an accessory to the murder, was acquitted, but Hanks wasn't so lucky. Originally, he was sentenced to be hanged and his body then taken to be dissected; but it was later changed to what was seen as a 'better' punishment for the man – to be hanged in chains near his own house, the scene of the crime.[16]

Some prisoners chose to take drastic means to avoid being executed by the hangman. On 17 March 1777, Joseph Armstrong, a Cheltenham servant, was tried at Gloucester Assizes for petty treason. He had allegedly poisoned Mrs A'Court, the wife of his employer, Captain A'Court. Mrs A'Court had often spoken of her dislike of Armstrong, and had tried to persuade her husband to dismiss the servant. Armstrong had learned of this, procured some arsenic from a local apothecary, and started regularly pouring drops of the poison into her beer and cups of tea over a period of ten days – at the end of which, Mrs A'Court died.

Only after her death did the apothecary come forward with a memory of having sold the arsenic to Armstrong. The latter then fled, pursued by Mrs A'Court's father, Colonel Bradford, who eventually caught up with the servant in woods at Frogmill, between Shipton Oliffe and Andoversford.[17]

Armstrong was found guilty of her murder, and sentenced to be hanged. However, while waiting for his sentence to be carried out, he devised another

Frogmill. Joseph Armstrong hid in the woods here.

plan, whereby he would take charge of his fate. His mother came to visit him in Gloucester Castle, bringing with her a small strap that she secretly passed to her son.

At 7 a.m. on the Monday morning, before he was due to be hanged, Armstrong asked the prison keepers to give him a couple of minutes on his own to pray. After securing his chains, they left him alone. Joseph Armstrong tied the little strap around his neck, fastened the end to a nail in the cell wall, and jerked his neck so suddenly that he dislocated it and died.[18]

Shortly before he killed himself, he had acknowledged both his part in the death of Mrs A'Court, and other previous crimes that would also have merited the death sentence had he been discovered to be the culprit.

Armstrong had been sentenced to be hung in chains after his execution, and this part of his sentence was still carried out; he was duly hung near the A'Courts' home in Cheltenham.[19]

These cases were not isolated instances; throughout the eighteenth century there are regular reports in the Calendars of Prisoners of men – and the occasional woman - being sentenced to be hung in chains.

The practice decreased in popularity as time went on, though, with the last recorded cases of being hanged in chains being in County Durham and Leicestershire in 1832. The sentence was abolished two years later.

There were other methods of ensuring that condemned men's bodies were humiliated after death, and one in particular was seen as providing further medical training for surgeons and anatomists. One case in the 1820s illustrates how those convicted of murder could receive a punishment that didn't just end with their hanging.

On 30 July 1824, two West Oxfordshire men stood trial for murder. The men were Henry Pittaway, a twenty-five-year-old labourer from Swinbrook, a village that then bordered the Wychwood Forest, who was married with two children; and forty-eight-year-old William James of Burford. James had been a slater and plasterer based in Taynton, and was married with six children. James found it hard to maintain his wife and large family, and had got into the habit of poaching venison from Wychwood Forest. He had been in Oxford Castle, convicted of poaching, on two former occasions, receiving a six month and a twelve-month prison sentence. He had then, in 1819, gone to gaol under the Vagrant Act for three months. After this conviction, neighbours and local gamekeepers viewed him with suspicion – they thought his poverty

The Swan at Swinbrook was home to Henry Pittaway.

St John's Church, Burford. The
town was home to William James.

Oxford Castle.

The Shaven Crown, formerly the Crown Inn, in Shipton-under-Wychwood.

might lead him to steal food from elsewhere. However, he also received some charity from locals; one farmer, Edward Colgrave of Swinbrook, had given him a whole sheep to feed his family with on one occasion.

This charitable move, though, caused more trouble; when gamekeeper James Millin passed James' door, and spied the meat, he assumed it was poached venison, and ensured that James was sent before the magistrates. He was subsequently freed without charge, but it shows the suspicion with which he was viewed in his community. It also shows that James may have had a grudge against the local gamekeeper.

James Millin, known by his family as Jem, had been on duty in the Wychwood Forest on the evening of 15 June, along with his brother Joseph. They had been patrolling separate areas, and at about 8.40 p.m. Joseph heard a gun being fired. Shortly afterwards, as he tried to locate where the sound had come from, he saw James and Pittaway walking towards Asthall. Pittaway said that he had heard a shot, and a halloo of 'Murder!' James said he thought the shot had come from the direction of Hensgrove, and the voice had sounded like James Millin's. The two poachers continued walking, but then stopped at a gap in a coppice. When Joseph Millin caught up with them, he found them standing by his brother, who was lying bleeding from a gunshot wound to his thigh. Pittaway was sent to South Lawn Lodge in Taynton, home of Lord Redesdale, to fetch help; he returned with a Mr Young and some of Young's friends, who carried Millin back to the lodge – where he died.

Three days later, the two men were overheard talking in the Crown Inn in Shipton-under-Wychwood. Local man George Hodgkins heard James say, 'Two men cannot be hung for one, as only one man can pull the trigger.' Others had heard James discuss violence and murder before the shooting occurred. After Millin's death, Pittaway's house was searched, and bullets were found matching the one used to shoot James Millin.

The two men were arrested, and charged with murder. The jury at their trial took fifteen minutes to find them guilty – the verdict apparently causing 'an audible sensation' in the court. The judge told the pair:

> The sentence of the Court upon you is that you, for this dreadful murder, be executed on Monday morning, and your bodies be afterwards given to the surgeons to be anatomised.

On Monday, 2 August 1824, at 6.45 a.m., Pittaway and James were led into the chapel of Oxford Castle and prepared for their deaths by the chaplain, who administered the sacrament to them. At 9 a.m. they were led to the scaffold, erected outside the castle. A large but quiet crowd had assembled to watch. As the rope was adjusted round Henry Pittaway's neck, James said, 'the rope is tight enough for me already, but I suppose it will soon be tighter!' – and then they were both hanged and left on the scaffold for several hours. When they were cut down, their bodies were taken to Oxford Gaol's surgeon, Mr Wentworth, who duly dissected and anatomised them.[20]

## Notes

[1] St Mary's Church history, accessed via
http://www.stmaryscnorton.com/church-history.html
[2] Capital Punishment UK, accessed via
http://www.capitalpunishmentuk.org/gloucester.html

[3] Nell Darby (2009), pp 83-90

[4] *Gloucester Journal*, 12 September 1732

[5] Nell Darby (2009), pp 27-32

[6] *Gloucester Journal*, 27 March 1744

[7] Joan Johnson (1994), p. 59

[8] *Gloucester Journal*, 7 November 1732

[9] *Gloucester Journal*, 28 April 1744

[10] Ross Harrison (1983), p. 6

[11] The Newgate Calendar, accessed via
http://www.exclassics.com/newgate/ng17.htm

[12] Burford Post Office history, accessed via
http://www.burfordpostoffice.co.uk/Tom-Dick--and--Harry.php

[13] The Belfast News-Letter, 17 June 1899, repeated in http://www.the-kirbys.
org.uk/gen/Places/Widford/GenealogyNotes.html

[14] The Wychwood Brewery,
http://www.wychwood.co.uk/#/world//hobgoblin/legends

[15] *Gloucester Journal*, 15 August 1727

[16] *Gloucester Journal*, 14 March 1763

[17] *Gloucester Journal*, 30 September 1776

[18] *Gloucester Journal*, 17 March 1777

[19] *Gloucester Journal*, 17 March 1777

[20] All quotes from *Jackson's Oxford Journal*, 7 August 1824

# 3

# BRANDING

In the eighteenth century, the punishment of being burned, or branded, was still legal – a remnant of the traditions of the Middle Ages. In Tudor times, branding was handed down as a punishment for any offence that received benefit of clergy – a visible sign that this defence, whereby an offender could show that he or she could recite a passage from the Bible, had already been used. Branding throughout the centuries had been used on various parts of the body – on the forehead, the breast, the thumb, the cheek, and the hand. It could be inflicted for various crimes, such as larceny, petty theft (for larger thefts, hanging or transportation was the punishment), or blasphemy.

Branding could be inflicted via a hot or a cold set of branding irons, with the initial of the crime forming the branded mark. The punishment served a dual purpose; firstly, it was incredibly painful, and thus served as a deterrent to committing further crimes; and secondly, the visibility of the branded mark would serve to humiliate the punished for a long time after the initial crime had been committed, singling them out for attention in their communities.

In practice, branding doesn't seem to have been carried out very often in the Cotswolds. In the first half of the eighteenth century, branding as a punishment was mainly handed down to those who were convicted at the assizes of manslaughter. For example, in July 1724, William White of Wotton-under-Edge, just west of the Cotswold Hills, was tried at the Summer Assizes for the murder of one Thomas Parry. White had stabbed him under his right arm with a knife after the two had quarrelled over a woman. As Parry had hit White twice in the face before being stabbed, White was found guilty only of manslaughter, and therefore sentenced to being burnt in the hand, rather than being hanged.[1]

In the 1720s, two people were branded on the hand at Gloucester Castle after being convicted of manslaughter, and Abraham Andrews was also branded after being convicted of manslaughter in April 1728.[2] In 1731, Thomas Clare, of Frogmill, was sentenced to be branded on the hand after being found guilty of the manslaughter of the wonderfully named John Wayne. He had been originally charged with murder, but only found guilty of the lesser offence.[3]

A year later, in March 1732, John Giles, who was from Compton Abdale and also known as John Child, appeared at the assizes with Margaret Goulding, accused of murdering Edward Dyer Jr. Margaret seems to have been acquitted, but John was found guilty of manslaughter after the court heard that he had struck Edward two blows to his head with a stick, the cause of his death. He was burned in the hand and then sent to Gloucester Gaol for eleven months[4]. Another two men – Thomas Burchell and William Moulder – were branded on the hand at Gloucester on 26 August 1732,[5] Burchell for the murder of John Causon. He had apparently been found guilty some time earlier, but had absconded; but at the beginning of March, he surrendered himself to the keeper of Gloucester Castle.[6]

Twenty years later, the punishment was still being inflicted for manslaughter; Stow-on-the-Wold resident Thomas Smith was sentenced to being burnt in the hand on 15 March 1746, after being convicted of manslaughter.[7] He had been brought to Gloucester Castle on 1 February, accused of stabbing John Taylor, possibly from Cutsdean, near Ford, after a row in a Stow public house.[8] Another man, James Ballinger, was also branded in August of that year,[9] and a couple more in 1750 and 1751.

Being branded on the hand.
(© Carolyn Ford and used with permission)

Gloucester Prison.

Thomas Smith lived in
Stow-on-the-Wold.

A pair of branding irons.

Women could also be sentenced to be branded, such as Elizabeth Gough in 1729. She was married to the landlord of the Boarded House alehouse in Kingswood, near Bristol. When another woman, Mary Willis, who was six months' pregnant, had come to call her husband home from the alehouse on 5 October 1728, Elizabeth had seen red, assaulting the pregnant woman and, once she had fallen to the floor, stamping on her. Mary Willis died a few days later – along with her unborn child. Elizabeth's burst of temper was seen as an act of manslaughter rather than murder, and in April 1729, at the Gloucester Assizes, she was ordered to be burnt in the hand.[10]

By 1770, the punishment was given for lesser crimes, and, alongside punishments such as the pillory – was a form of public humiliation and therefore a deterrent to committing further crimes.[11] Originally, the branded mark was a letter representing the crime that had been committed – such as T for theft – and was made with an iron. The burn – and its subsequent scar – would have distinguished the criminal from the rest of society and marked them out as different. It was a permanent reminder of a dark episode in the unfortunate person's life.

The gaol records for Gloucester Castle show that at the Summer Assizes of 1771, Rachel Gregory was found guilty of burglary, and ordered to be 'burnt in the hand' and to be imprisoned at the castle for six months.[12] On 14 July 1778, it was noted that Jane Eldridge had been found guilty at the Lent Assizes of stealing goods and money. Initially, it seems that she was sentenced to hard labour in the House of Correction for one year and then discharged; but on 6 October 1778, a note was added that in addition to her twelve-month prison sentence she had also been burnt in the hand.[13]

Branding was abolished in 1829, except in the case of army deserters, who might still be branded or tattooed with a mark. But branding had, luckily for criminals, been quietly put aside as a punishment in the Cotswolds several decades earlier.

## Notes

[1] *Gloucester Journal*, 3 August 1724
[2] *Gloucester Journal*, 16 April 1728
[3] *Gloucester Journal*, 3 August 1731 and 10 August 1731
[4] *Gloucester Journal*, 7 March 1732 and 14 March 1732
[5] *Gloucester Journal*, 29 August 1732
[6] *Gloucester Journal*, 8 August 1732

[7] *Gloucester Journal*, 18 March 1746

[8] *Gloucester Journal*, 4 February 1746 [9] *Gloucester Journal*, 19 August 1746

[10] *Gloucester Journal*, 8 April August 1729

[11] 'Crime and Punishment', British Library, accessed via http://www.bl.uk/learning/histcitizen/georgians/crime/crimeandpunishment.html

[12] Calendar of Prisoners, Gloucestershire Archives, ref Q/SG/1/1771-9)

[13] Calendar of Prisoners, Gloucestershire Archives, ref Q/SG/1 1771-9

# 4

# IMPRISONMENT

Prison sentences in the eighteenth and nineteenth centuries could be, to modern eyes, quite random, but also quite harsh. Children were, until the latter part of the nineteenth century, held in adult prisons and treated no differently to those many times their age. In June 1833, for example, Moses Henry Rose, who was just ten years old, was convicted of stealing apples and sent to Northleach House of Correction for one month.[1]

Prison was intended to act as a deterrent to those who had committed crimes; therefore, prison life was made as intolerable as possible to ensure that people didn't make a return visit there. Judging by the frequency of names reappearing again and again in the Calendars of Prisoners, this aim was not, ultimately, very successful.

Prisoners might be sent to the main prison at Gloucester, which had opened in 1782, replacing the old Gloucester Castle, and which was rebuilt in 1840. However, for more minor crimes and shorter spells of imprisonment, they might be sent to one of Gloucestershire's Houses of Correction. These existed at Dursley, Lawford's Gate and Northleach. In Oxfordshire, the main prison and House of Correction was at Oxford Castle – now, ironically, a luxury hotel that publicises its penal origins - with other Houses of Correction being in the north – at Banbury – and south – at Thame. In the nineteenth century, local police stations such as the one still existing at Chipping Norton were also used to house and punish prisoners.

In the 1830s, a new form of punishment for those given prison sentences started to be used in Gloucestershire. In March 1835, twenty-year-old Richard Carpenter, convicted of stealing three chairs, was sentenced to '12 months in the penitentiary house, the last month solitude'.[2] The use of solitary confinement was frequently specified from 1835 in a judge's sentencing. In January 1836, sixteen-year-old Frederic Sawyer and nineteen-year-old Thomas Atwood were convicted of stealing a calico shirt from Richard Godwin in Lechlade. They were handed three-year prison sentences each, with the added request that they spend the last fortnight of their sentences in solitary confinement.[3]

Some rebelled against their imprisonment and tried to escape or protest in some way. In the House of Correction at Lawford's Gate, the other side of Gloucester to Northleach, an eighteen-year-old man named John Wakefield had been sentenced to death after 'riotously assembling with others and setting fire to the House of Correction' in 1832.[4] Although Northleach was never subject to arson, some prisoners did try to escape – and were subsequently further punished.

Other prisoners saw prison as a humiliation, or, when held on remand there, feared the ultimate sentence they would receive so much that they were driven to take their own lives. In April 1828, *Berrow's Worcester Journal* recorded the case of Ann Hamerton, a milliner from Tewkesbury, who had been living in Cheltenham. Described as a 'very genteel-looking young woman, of engaging appearance', Ann was charged with stealing a £10 bank note and clothes from an elderly lady named Mary Davis, whom she had been staying with. Ann then issued a charge against Miss Davis for falsely accusing her. Davis was sent, despite her age, to Northleach House of Correction; when further information came in, police re-arrested Ann Hamerton. She was tried, found guilty, and sent to the County Gaol. During her first night in a cell, she managed to kill herself; initially it was thought that she had simply hanged herself using her silk handkerchief, but subsequently it was found that she had managed to strangle herself using 'voluntary exertions of the body' without suspending her body from her home-made noose.[5]

Prison conditions could be poor, and sentencing men to hard labour could mean giving them a death sentence. Conditions in Northleach House of Correction in the first half of the nineteenth century were notoriously bad, and after the death of one man, Charles Beale, in 1842, an inquiry was held into discipline and diet at the prison.

A report in *The Times* from the year of Charles Beale's death repeated the views of a prison inspector about Northleach's conditions two years earlier:

A prison cell at Northleach
House of Correction.

Lechlade, where two teenagers committed a theft in 1835.

Cheltenham, where milliner Ann Hamerton lived.

> The prisoners…pass the whole day either at the tread-wheel or locked up in their cells, except for one hour and a half; and on Sundays are locked up the whole day, except during two hours and a half, and when they attend chapel. They eat in their cells.[6]

In addition, the prisoners weren't allowed any visits or letters during the first six months of their imprisonment. When they were finally allowed letters, they were only given the ones deemed to be important – other correspondence was withheld from them until their release. *The Times* stated that solitary confinement at Northleach consisted of six hours at a time in a dark cell (with the note that the short period of time was due to the fact that 'the cells are damp'). Whilst in the cells, prisoners were not allowed any books to read, had only bread and water to sustain them, and one hour's exercise a day.

So prisoners had a meagre, repetitive diet, were kept in damp cells, and had little opportunity for socialising or exercise. After Beale's death, the *Bristol Mercury* stated:

It is absolutely horrible to reflect that a poor wretch, who, perhaps under the pressure of poverty, has committed some trifling offence, shall be sent, while in full health, into a prison, where, by the privations inflicted upon him, he shall imbibe the seeds of consumption, and be sent out again upon the world reduced to the verge of death, and, even if disposed, incapable from debility to earn his bread by his honest labour.[7]

A correspondent for the *Morning Chronicle*, a long-term resident of Cheltenham, who had frequently visited Northleach, described it as 'without exception, one of the most damp, loathsome dungeons in England.'[8] This correspondent quoted a Cheltenham man who, incarcerated in Northleach, had written to a friend:

For God's sake, try to get me liberated from this horrid place, which will shorten my days – if I don't shortly get out I shall die of starvation. They scarcely allow sufficient food to keep soul and body together; the gaol is wretchedly damp, although the weather is so warm. You have no idea of my sufferings.[9]

One of the things that emerged from the inquiry into conditions at Northleach was the practice of the gaolers to cut the prisoners' hair so short that it 'disfigured' them. This was an additional punishment, designed to humiliate them, and make them stand out as prisoners. At the Epiphany Sessions in Gloucester in 1843, a visiting justices' report on Northleach was presented. In it, the justices ordered that 'in future none but the turnkey should cut the prisoners' hair, that it should not be cut so close as to disfigure their persons, but merely sufficiently so for the purpose of cleanliness, and to serve as a mark in case of escape.'[10] The authorities wanted prisoners to look different to law-abiding members of society.

Of course, the danger was that for men given the option of a prison sentence or a fine, that they might have their hair shorn as soon as they were sent to prison, and if they then paid their fine - it might, after all, take a bit of time to arrange for someone to come with the money and pay it - they could find themselves legally free, but still with a convict's haircut, which might hinder their attempts to find or continue work. So a provision was made that in cases where paying a fine was given as an alternative punishment, a prisoner wouldn't have his hair cut until he had served two or three days in prison, just in case the fine was paid within this time.[11]

Charles Beale's wasn't the last death at Northleach. In April 1843, an inquest was held into the death of Richard Jones, aged only eighteen, who was also an inmate of the House of Correction. At his inquest, the jury repeatedly stated that 'the hard work and scanty food of the prison was the cause of the evil' but also that 'it was the system, and not the particular individuals who administered the law' that was to blame for the deaths at Northleach.[12] Another man, Joseph King, who had just been released from Northleach, was called on to give evidence at the inquest. He caused a 'great sensation' amongst the jury as he 'seemed little more than a living skeleton, and was evidently in the last stage of decline. His age was twenty-two years.'[13]

Evidence was heard that Jones had complained to the prison governor, Richard Townsend, that he felt 'dreadfully ill'. The governor's response was to tell him to go to work, or be locked up in his cell. He then complained to Ralph Bedwell, the prison's surgeon, who said the same. He was put on the treadwheel, but was so frail that he fell off it. The governor then responded, 'Jones, you are deceiving us to get out of the flogging, but you shall not escape'.[14] However, intervention by the surgeon meant that the sentence was dispensed with.

Another prisoner said he had seen the under-turnkey shoving Jones around and accusing him of 'shamming', despite the prisoner having to walk doubled up, crying, with a pain in his side so bad that he couldn't stand upright on the treadwheel. The under-turnkey told Jones, 'I will make you remember Northleach as long as you live' – an example of how some members of prison staff were gratuitously violent towards their charges. As a result of the Northleach inquiry, the under-turnkey was sacked from his post, and the governor reprimanded – he retired shortly afterwards.

However, a change in staff didn't improve matters; in 1845, there was a further case where an inmate died after being mistreated at Northleach – the prison continued to be a *cause celebre* in both the local and national press throughout the 1840s.

The treadwheel was the main form of both exercise and punishment for the prisoners. Commonly used during the early Victorian period as an additional punishment to merely being in prison, prisoners would be expected to walk thousands of feet on the treadwheel, spending hours walking and walking. As the Jones case showed, men were expected to take part in this monotonous activity regardless of their physical health. Starved on a meagre diet (they often had nothing to eat from 2 p.m. until 8 a.m. the next day,[15]) they then expended calories that they couldn't afford to lose on the activity. When they were brought off it, their shirts were dripping with sweat, which rapidly cooled. Still in these shirts, they were then sent straight to their damp cells. It is no wonder

The treadwheel.

that many prisoners at Northleach complained of consumptive symptoms. Richard Townsend said that there was only a budget of three shillings a week to buy meat to feed the prisoners with, which was only enough to make a thin soup. Disobeying the prison rules was also, he said, punished with extra rounds on the treadwheel, regardless of the prisoner's health.

It was found at Jones's inquest that although he died of consumption – aggravated by the prison conditions – he was also emaciated, covered in sores, and his death may have been accelerated by 'mental depression' over his treatment. This shows another side-effect, or additional punishment, caused by prison sentencing – the effect of incarceration on a prisoner's mental health. There was little mental or physical stimulation, little sustenance, and nothing to look at to relieve the monotony. Under such conditions, prisoners suffered. A prison sentence was something to be feared, and with good reason.

A sad postscript to life at Northleach House of Correction; it wasn't just the prisoners who suffered mentally whilst incarcerated. At the beginning of 1847, the prison chaplain, Revd Ireland, was found dead in his bedroom, having cut his throat. He had only been working at the prison for four months, having previously been chaplain at the Malmesbury Poor Law Union. He was elderly and poor, for a chaplain's pay wasn't great. He had appealed to the Gloucestershire magistrates to be paid his salary quarterly,

Malmesbury, once home of the unfortunate Revd Ireland.

in advance, to help him out. They didn't have the power to do this, so had to decline. Ireland, in poverty, and with a wife and seven children to support, killed himself.[16]

Not all criminals were concerned about life in Northleach House of Correction, despite its grim history. In 1849, Thomas Roberts, a Tewkesbury labourer, was convicted of breaking Mr Grizzle's shop window in Kemerton, the result of a bet with friends. He was sentenced to one month's imprisonment in Northleach, but *Berrow's Worcester Journal* reported, 'The prisoner asked to be immured for a considerably longer period, but this request was not acceded to'.[17] Perhaps the prison diet, however poor, was better than Roberts got at home; or perhaps he simply wanted a break from the friends who had bet on him to break Grizzle's window.

Others were imprisoned for personal decisions that had financial implications for their parish. Where a man left his wife and/or children – either to seek temporary work elsewhere or as a permanent separation – a parish would seek a warrant for his arrest, on the grounds that the remaining family had sought poor relief and therefore cost it money. In September 1836, for example, Ann Green, a thirty-one-year-old mother of four from Didbrook, applied for relief nine weeks after her husband had absconded. He had left to seek work on the railways in Birmingham, and had told his wife he would return shortly with his wages. She, in the meantime, was left penniless. The Winchcombe authorities allowed her a shilling in money and four shillings' worth of bread for a week, but on a strictly loan basis. They then asked for a warrant to be obtained from the local constable to arrest

Didbrook, where Ann Green and her children lived.

Charles Green for leaving Ann and their children, Elizabeth (nine), Charles (seven), William (four), and Sarah (two), chargeable to the parish.[18]

When Charles was brought back – his arrest costing the parish constable, George Hawkes, over £4 – he was promptly committed to the local bridewell for three weeks. Of course, this meant he was no longer earning, and a week after his arrest, Ann had to apply again for relief, this time obtaining two shillings.[19] Ann, close to giving birth to her fifth child, had to seek further relief over the next two weeks. Her husband was then released from prison, and her parish money was immediately stopped, it being assumed that Charles Green would immediately step into another job and take on financial responsibility for his family.[20]

Another Cotswolds woman, Mary Lock, of Stanway, suffered in a similar way when her husband was sent to prison for a felony. At twenty-eight, she had three children – Mary (six), Sarah (five), and five-month-old baby Thomas, and was unable to maintain them with her husband in prison not earning. She was awarded three shillings of money and three shillings' worth of bread per week until further notice after she applied for relief from the Winchcombe Poor Law Board.[21]

It is evident that imprisonment was tough, involving back-breaking or monotonous work, often in poor conditions and risking health or life. Men, women and children were incarcerated for a wide range of crimes, some of which were committed out of financial necessity. And for those committed to prison or the local lock-up for trying to find work outside their parishes, it was often their innocent families who suffered, forced to live on the poverty line while their partners were behind bars.

## Notes

[1] Calendar of Prisoners, Gloucestershire Archives, reference Q/SG/2/1833

[2] Calendar of Prisoners, Gloucestershire Archives, reference Q/SG/2/1835

[3] Calendar of Prisoners, Gloucestershire Archives, reference Q/SG/2/ Epiphany Sessions 5 January 1836

[4] Calendar of Prisoners, Gloucestershire Archives, reference Q/SG/2/1832

[5] *Berrow's Worcester Journal*, 17 April 1828

[6] *The Times*, 12 October 1842, p. 4

[7] *Bristol Mercury*, 8 October 1842

[8] *Morning Chronicle*, 28 October 1842

[9] *Morning Chronicle*, 28 October 1842

[10] *Morning Chronicle*, 6 January 1843

[11] *Morning Chronicle*, 6 January 1843

[12] *Morning Chronicle*, 13 April 1843

[13] *Morning Chronicle*, 13 April 1843

[14] *Morning Chronicle*, 13 April 1843

[15] *Jackson's Oxford Journal*, 22 April 1843

[16] *The Era*, 7 February 1847

[17] *Berrow's Worcester Journal*, 1 November 1849

[18] Meetings of the Winchcombe Poor Law Board, 10 September 1836, Gloucestershire Archives reference G/WI/8a/1

[19] Meetings of the Winchcombe Poor Law Board, 24 September 1836 and 1 October 1836, Gloucestershire Archives reference G/WI/8a/1

[20] Meetings of the Winchcombe Poor Law Board, 8 October 1836 and 15 October 1836, Gloucestershire Archives reference G/WI/8a/1

[21] Meetings of the Winchcombe Poor Law Board, 20 February 1836, Gloucestershire Archives reference G/WI/8a/1

# 5

# TRANSPORTATION

Transportation was a common punishment in the 1600s and 1700s, serving the purpose of getting rid of those seen to be a menace to British society (out of sight, out of mind) and providing labour to the burgeoning society in America.

Although transportation had started in 1615, it wasn't until the 1718 Transportation Act that transportation to America for seven years for those convicted of non-capital offences, or fourteen years (for those entitled to conditional pardons[1]) became a legally proscribed punishment. Transportation was usually to New England at this stage. Two years later, a revision to the Act permitted payments to merchants from the State, to enable them to ship convicts to the colonies.

Convicts were expected to work – provided, of course, that they survived the long boat journey across the Atlantic. Male convicts might have to work in American mines or on road building schemes; female convicts might work as servants to settlers. Removing convicts from their homes was seen as a more humane punishment than execution, but one that would deter those on fixed-time transportation punishments – usually seven years – from committing another crime once they returned home. Anyone who managed to escape and tried to return to Britain could be punished with the death sentence; conversely, some people convicted of death could have their sentences reduced to transportation. Even when the evidence against prisoners was slight, a sentence might be reduced to transportation rather than a full pardon being given, such as in the case of Henry Emms, convicted at Gloucester Assizes in 1727 of highway robbery and sentenced to death. The evidence against him was, said his judge, 'slight and weak', and so he was transported to America instead.[2]

By the middle of the eighteenth century, it was believed that the sentence of transportation had lost its fearful connotations for prisoners. David Taylor has written that America was becoming more accessible from Britain, due to the development of faster boats, so that criminals knew they would be able to reach home once their sentences were over.[3]

However, the courts continued to send convicts to the American colonies. An undated document in the National Archives, probably from the early 1770s, shows how several Gloucestershire men convicted of capital offences had their sentences commuted to transportation. These included John Marrott and Jarvis Harris, who had been convicted of carrying out a burglary together, and who had originally been given the death sentence. They were then reprieved on condition that they were transported to America for seven years.[4]

Several others were convicted of animal stealing at the Gloucester Assizes at around the same time – again a capital offence during this era. Robert Hulbert was convicted of horse stealing; Samuel Griffin of sheep stealing. Both had their death sentences commuted to seven years in America. These reprieves came as a result of what was described as 'favourable circumstances' in their cases that merited them being given mercy.[5]

Transportation to America ended when war broke out between the two nations in 1776, and an alternative destination needed to be found. Australia was the solution, and transportation to Botany Bay in New South Wales started in 1787, with the first convict ship arriving at Port Jackson in January 1788.

Within two years, Gloucestershire was sending many convicts Down Under, of all ages. In July 1789, eighteen-year-old Hester Vevas was convicted of a felony and given a sentence of seven years' transportation. However, it could take time to arrange the transportation, and two years later, Hester was still in Gloucester Gaol, waiting to be sent to Australia.[6]

Transportation at the end of the eighteenth century in the Cotswolds could be given for various lengths – usually seven years, fourteen years, or for life. In 1798, thirty-year-old Thomas Robinson was convicted of 'sacrilege' and told to be transported to the eastern coast of New South Wales 'for and during the term of his natural life'.[7] At the same time, twenty-two-year old William Hogg received the same sentence for stealing over forty shillings'

Cotswold sheep. Sheep stealing was punished with transportation.

worth of goods from a house; and eighteen-year-old John Marsh received transportation for life for house-breaking.[8]

An alternative punishment to transportation sometimes handed down in late eighteenth-century courts was that of working on the River Thames in order to improve navigation – these convicts were some of the original 'navvies'. In the summer of 1776, for example, Stephen Teakle was convicted of stealing silk breeches, velvet breeches, a waistcoat and some Holland shirts from the home of one John Harris. He was ordered to be 'kept to hard labour upon the navigation of the River Thames for three years and then to be discharged'.[9] In 1777, George Cox was convicted of stealing a sack belonging to one Edward Winter, and had to work on the Thames for four years. At the same time, John Pritchard was sentenced to three years' navigation work and Richard Chew and Robert Hill six years each.[10] In 1779, Edward Nail was convicted at the Summer Assizes in Gloucester of a felony, and ordered to 'work upon the Thames for five years for the use of the navigation there.'[11] However, these sentences were rare and seem to have only been handed out during the 1770s.

By the start of the nineteenth century, with another penal colony being established in Tasmania, transportation was being given as a punishment more often – coinciding with legal reformer Sir Samuel Romilly's removal of the death penalty for lesser crimes in 1808, and an increase in the number

The River Thames, where Cotswold prisoners could be sent to work.

of death sentences being commuted. Twenty-five-year-old Samuel Clift received fourteen years' transportation in 1801 for receiving stolen goods, and he was not a unique case. Twenty-two-year-old Sarah Haynes received transportation for life for house-breaking the same year; thirty-nine-year-old Charlotte Holland received the same sentence for forgery.

The same punishment was given for an array of offences – from one man being convicted of 'shooting at one of his Majesty's subjects' in 1810[12] to another convicted of shoplifting.

After this period, the number of transportations dramatically decreased, with only a couple being given each year. However, from 1820, the numbers increased again.

In the Cotswolds, transportation was a common form of punishment at this time. In fact, there was little difference between the crimes and punishments of these early nineteenth-century offenders, and those less than a century earlier – except that America had been replaced by Australia as the destination for those punished by a sentence of transportation.

On New Year's Day 1822, twenty-five-year-old Thomas Poulton was transported for seven years after stealing a till containing eight shillings from John Smith, a Cirencester druggist.[13] Later the same year, Charles Smith – the same age as Poulton – was convicted of stealing the skin of a ewe from an Upper Slaughter farm and was transported for the same period.[14]

Upper Slaughter, the home of
Charles Smith.

Northleach, the setting for both
crimes and punishment.

Eighteen-year-old William Paget was transported for seven years for stealing shoes, garters and a smock frock from a stable in Widford in 1826,[15] and twenty-two-year-old Richard Wheeler was given the same sentence for stealing gilt seals and a few thimbles from John Beal's shop in Fairford.[16] A year later, thirty-one-year-old Calvin Sansum stole John Sealey's hat from him in Tetbury, and was also transported.[17]

And the Cotswold transportations continued. In July 1829, twenty-year-old Joseph Davis and thirty-two-year-old Ambrose Minchin broke into George Day's coachhouse in Northleach and stole some silver cutlery belonging to Lt-Col. Philip Clarke. They were transported for seven years.[18] So too was Richard Spencer, aged just sixteen, who was convicted of stealing two boxes of cakes from a Mr and Mrs Debank in Northleach.[19] Twenty-three-year-old Jasper Hale was transported for seven years after stealing a 'lees-dropper' from the hovel adjoining his house in Kemble. Despite the building being neglected, the owner, William Burgess, still prosecuted Hale.[20]

In 1830, the Swing Riots took place across England, as agricultural workers protested against the use of machinery in farming. Gloucester saw many trials of rioters who had destroyed threshing machines, chaff machines, or

Coln St Aldwyns, one of the Swing Riot locations.

other pieces of equipment at farms in the Cotswolds. The authorities were scared of working-class unhappiness, and the power of mass protests, and so sought to stamp on these miscreants by handing down heavy punishments – yet the punishments given varied greatly.

The Epiphany Sessions in January 1831 dealt with the many men – and a couple of women – charged with destroying threshing machines in Fairford, Quenington, Beverstone and Coln St Aldwyns. Thomas Weaving, James Silk and Joseph Edgington were convicted of destroying threshing machines belonging to farmer Robert Price and paper maker Joshua Corby Radway, both of Quenington, and received seven-year transportation sentences, as did Elizabeth Parker, convicted of 'assisting in riot of people who destroyed the threshing machine of Jacob Hayward of Beverstone'.[21] However, three others – William Debank, John Kent and Edward Whitehead – were acquitted of destroying three machines in Coln St Aldwyns; and Thomas Turner and James Fox, although convicted of breaking a threshing machine at the same sessions, were imprisoned for twelve months at Northleach House of Correction, but weren't given a transportation sentence.

William Paget, transported for stealing clothes, was from the hamlet of Widford.

Transportation was seen as a suitable punishment for those who disrupted the social order. Rioting and protesting about aspects of one's employment was seen as a dangerous thing to permit – the working classes had to be kept in check. So just as some of those convicted of taking part in the Swing Riots were sentenced to be sent to Australia, so too were others who tried to escape from their existing confines; for example, twenty-six-year-old Edmund Morgan escaped from the Northleach House of Correction in 1835 after being convicted of a felony – and was subsequently sentenced to seven years' transportation for that escape attempt.[22]

The increase in numbers from 1820 heralded what David Taylor asserts to be the national peak in transportations to Australia in the 1830s;[23] although, of course, that wouldn't take into account the numbers who were sentenced to transportation but ended up spending their time in British prisons or prison hulks before being released, or who died before they could be transported. In fact, many people didn't get transported, despite their sentence. By the mid-1800s, transportation was still often the punishment for what we would consider to be minor crimes today – but it was rarely carried out in practice. It cost money and resources to arrange for convicts to be transported to the other side of the world, and so some served their sentence without setting foot outside the country.

On 15 October 1850, at the Quarter Sessions in Gloucester, twenty-year-old Richard Frederick Gregory was convicted of stealing pigs and sentenced to seven years' transportation. However, Richard, a native of Stratford-upon-Avon, who was variously described as a shoemaker or a labourer, was actually listed as a convict at the St Loyes Street County Prison in Bedford in 1851, and was then sent to Dartmoor Prison. He was given early release from there on 10 April 1854.[24]

The National Archives show that many men convicted of stealing or obtaining goods by false pretences in the 1850s were given seven or ten years' transportation, but in fact ended up serving only a few years in an English prison before being released.

Those convicted of more serious offences were no less likely to stay in the country; Thomas Stephens, a twenty-one-year-old coal miner convicted at Gloucester of rape on 9 August 1851, was sentenced to fifteen years' transportation, but ended up serving just under seven years at Portsmouth; a year earlier, George White, a twenty-four-year-old post office clerk convicted of stealing a letter that contained money, was sentenced to seven years' transportation, but ended up serving three years in Dartmoor Prison before being released early on licence.[25]

The average sentence of men sentenced to transportation at Gloucester in the late 1840s and early '50s seems to have been around three or four years. Theft was the most common offence that these men – and, less commonly, women – were convicted of, from stealing a duck (William Miles in 1850[26]) to lead from a church (John Spencer, the same year[27]).

Cotswold men were also ordered to spend time on the prison hulks. This was nothing new; for example, in 1784, Gloucestershire man Isaac Jason was convicted of housebreaking, and after being originally sentenced to death, was reprieved and ordered on board the prison hulk *Justitia* for five years' hard labour. On 12 June 1789, he was freed and given an outfit of 'decent clothing' after the convicts' overseer, Duncan Campbell, reported to the King's Bench that Jason had served most of his sentence, and with good conduct.[28] The difference between Isaac Jason's case, though, and those of the 1850s was that in the 1780s, Jason's death sentence was commuted straight to hard labour; in the nineteenth century, a sentence of transportation was commuted to hard labour on the hulks.

One example was twenty-five-year-old Edward Parry, a labourer convicted of burglary on 29 March 1851, who spent three years on the *Defence* hulk before being released on licence on 28 August 1854.[29] This may be the same Edward Parry, born in Manchester, who was listed as a prisoner at Gloucester Gaol in the 1851 census, although he is recorded as being a journeyman fishmonger. Henry Gloucester (eighteen) was sentenced to ten years' transportation in 1851 after being convicted of burglary. The increased tariff was due to having a previous conviction for a felony. He served four years on the *Stirling Castle* hulk before being released.[30]

A whole group of men sentenced at Gloucester in 1840 were sent together to the prison hulk *Leviathan*, moored at Portsmouth. Twenty-four-year-old labourer Richard Taylor, thirty-year-old James Alexander, and fifty-nine-year-old John Woodruff, alias Groves, were sent there after being convicted of horse stealing and having received the sentence of transportation for life. Woodruff had previously been sentenced to seven years' transportation for a previous offence, and all three were given the character reference 'bad – convicted before' in the Prison Hulk registers.[31]

They were held along with other Gloucestershire men, including John Brunson Avery, a forty-year-old baker convicted of 'forging and uttering a deed with intent to defraud', who had previously served a two-year sentence for another crime, and who was now serving a ten-year transportation sentence. Like James Alexander and John Woodruff, Avery was married,

Prison hulk *The Warrior*.

and had to leave his wife to look after the family financially. In an age of increasing literacy, all but Richard Taylor – whose reading and writing was listed as being 'imperfect' – were literate men.

The *Leviathan* was an old ship, having been built in 1790, and conditions must have been poor on board. The ship had been used during the Napoleonic wars, but had been a prison hulk since around 1816. It continued to be used in this way until finally being taken out of commission in 1846.[32]

Although some men were sent to the prison hulks, most were held at standard prisons – often Dartmoor, Portland or Portsmouth, although others were held at Parkhurst on the Isle of Wight, or Millbank in London. Eleven-year-old Charles Meek was convicted of stealing an oak desk on 12 January 1852, and sentenced to seven years' transportation. He ended up serving three years in Parkhurst Prison.[33]

The men sentenced to transportation were overwhelmingly from working-class backgrounds. Many were agricultural labourers; others were in trades, such as shoemaking, brickmaking, or stocking knitting. A more well-to-do man, hairdresser Charles Hughes, was convicted of burglary in 1849; the twenty-eight-year-old was given a sentence of fifteen years' transportation, but was released from Millbank seven years later.[34]

Transportation was becoming unpopular with the British public by this time and not seen as an appropriate deterrent for offenders. There was also an unevenness in how sentences were handed down. For example, in 1841, one Eliphalet Parsloe was sentenced to fifteen years' transportation after being convicted of stealing a sheep at Owlpen, the property of Thomas Anthony Stoughton, but at the same Assizes, Charles Mallard was convicted of assaulting a 'respectable' widow and mother-of-ten by filling her mouth with mud, throttling her and trying to rape her – but only received a two-year prison sentence.[35]

Parsloe's harsher sentence was partly due to the fact that he had a prior conviction against him, and the lack of regard given to women who were the victims of sexual crimes. However, the variety of sentences that could be handed down for wildly differing crimes, the fact that receiving these sentences did little to deter people from committing crime, and the sheer number of people being sentenced to transportation meant that it was unfeasible to continue to use it as a punishment. In 1867, transportation ended.

## Notes

[1] National Archives Research Guide, accessed via http://www. nationalarchives.gov.uk/records/research-guides/transportation-america-west-indies.htm

[2] National Archives reference SP36/2

[3] David Taylor (1998), p. 143

[4] National Archives reference HO 47/3/105

[5] National Archives reference HO 47/3/105

[6] Calendar of Prisoners, Gloucestershire Archives reference Q/SG/2/1798

[7] Calendar of Prisoners, Gloucestershire Archives reference Q/SG/2/1798

[8] Calendar of Prisoners, Gloucestershire Archives reference Q/SG/2/1798

[9] Calendar of Prisoners, Gloucestershire Archives reference Q/SG/1/1776

[10] Calendar of Prisoners, Gloucestershire Archives reference Q/SG/1/1777

[11] Calendar of Prisoners, Gloucestershire Archives reference Q/SG/1/1779

[12] Calendar of Prisoners, Gloucestershire Archives reference Q/SG/2/1810

[13] Calendar of Prisoners, Gloucestershire Archives reference Q/SG/2/1822

[14] Calendar of Prisoners, Gloucestershire Archives reference Q/SG/2/1822

[15] Calendar of Prisoners, Gloucestershire Archives reference Q/SG/2/1827

[16] Calendar of Prisoners, Gloucestershire Archives reference Q/SG/2/1827

[17] Calendar of Prisoners, Gloucestershire Archives reference Q/SG/2/1828
[18] Calendar of Prisoners, Gloucestershire Archives reference Q/SG/2/1829
[19] Calendar of Prisoners, Gloucestershire Archives reference Q/SG/2/1830
[20] Calendar of Prisoners, Gloucestershire Archives, reference Q/SG/2/1830
[21] Calendar of Prisoners, Gloucestershire Archives, reference Q/SG/2/1831
[22] Calendar of Prisoners, Gloucestershire Archives, reference Q/SG/2/1835
[23] David Taylor (1998), p. 143
[24] National Archives reference PCOM 3/8/722
[25] National Archives reference PCOM 3/1/49
[26] National Archives reference PCOM 3/4/321
[27] National Archives reference PCOM 3/2/112
[28] National Archives reference HO 47/8/98 and HO 47/3/104
[29] National Archives reference PCOM/3/15/1522
[30] National Archives PCOM/3/39/4192
[31] Prison Hulk Registers, accessed via www.ancestry.co.uk
[32] http://www.kenscott.com/prisons/hulks.htm
[33] National Archives reference PCOM/3/29/2999
[34] National Archives reference PCOM 3/44/4802
[35] *Bristol Mercury*, 14 August 1841

# 6

# WHIPPING

It was believed, for much of the nineteenth century, that there was a criminal type, often able to be detected through someone's physiognomy. There was little sympathy for male offenders, as it was believed they came from the 'criminal class'.

Children who committed crimes, too, were seen as being naturally cunning and not to be empathised or sympathised with. In 1848, the *Morning Post* contained a piece headlined 'Cunning Juvenile Offenders', which reported a speech given by a Manchester magistrate, Mr Maude. Talking about the 1847 Juvenile Offenders Act that gave summary powers to justices in petty sessions to deal with larceny offences committed by children under fifteen, Maude complained:

> One of the penalties inflicted by the Act in question is that of privately whipping boys under fourteen years of age. Within a very short time after the Act became law, little urchins apprehended on charges of this description, though scarcely able to look over the dock, when asked by the magistrate their age, invariably answered, 'Going o' fifteen'.[1]

The Act enabled justices to imprison minors for up to three months, fine them, or arrange for them to be privately whipped. They would be whipped with a birch – a bunch of twigs bound together – that would sometimes be soaked in water or brine to make it both heavier and stronger.

In 1861, the Oxfordshire magistrates discussed the recent reduction in the local crime rate. The Right Honourable J.W. Henley MP spoke about another recently passed Act – probably the Larceny Act - regarding juvenile offenders:

> The punishment of whipping is confined to persons under sixteen years of age. I perceive there is one case which extends it to persons of eighteen years, but I think this is an error in the Act … The number of lashes, and the instrument to be used, are likewise fixed by the Act.[2]

Whipping as a punishment for boys was seen as acceptable, and even desirable, by the authorities, and they also saw parental discipline – in the form of physical punishments – as necessary to keep a child on the straight and narrow. A case in nearby Worcester in 1862 saw eleven-year-old William Tuggins charged with stealing a cap from a ten-year-old friend. Although the case was dismissed, the judge still 'recommended' that Mr and Mrs Tuggins 'give him a whipping'.[3]

Even in the late nineteenth century, whipping was still a common punishment for juveniles convicted of minor crimes, usually given in conjunction with a short custodial sentence. In 1873, for example, fourteen-year-old Cheltenham boy Charles Evans was convicted at Southwark of stealing two pairs of boots, and sentenced to three days' hard labour and a whipping.[4] Charles was convicted of larceny under the Juvenile Offenders Act. Another boy convicted the same month – thirteen-year-old James Hempson – had stolen a box of figs, and received four days' hard labour together with being 'whipped 10 strokes with birch'.[5]

The couple of months, or even years, of hard labour that adult criminals received for theft was deemed unsuitable for children – but whipping and a couple of days in prison were seen as a perfectly reasonable alternative. However, money also came into the equation. It was cheaper to whip a child and give him a few days' detention than incur the expense of holding him in the House of Correction for longer.

In 1830, the Home Office received a letter from a Mr Huntingford, arguing that instead of sending beggars to the House of Correction, at public expense, they should instead simply be 'summarily whipped'.[6] The government's and public's desire to save money, and free up the resources of the quarter sessions and assizes, was undoubtedly a factor in sentencing minor offenders to such a punishment.

The former police station at Winchcombe. Public whipping may have taken place in the town.

There seemed to be far less argument about the form of punishment than about how it should be administered. MPs debated where whippings should be carried out, whether the punishment should only be given for a second or subsequent offence, and how many strokes of the birch offenders should receive.

Of course, it wasn't just children who were liable to be whipped for transgressions. In 1800, there was allegedly a case in Winchcombe, where six women were found guilty of hedge-pulling. This offence could mean either the deliberate destruction of hedges in a political act intended to stop or delay the enclosure of fields, or the economic need to obtain firewood from hedgerows. The women were apparently sentenced to be stripped to the waist and flogged. Unfortunately, I have been unable to find evidence of this sentence, as some of the relevant prisoner records for this time haven't survived, but there was often a whipping post in villages and towns, where offenders were locked in irons before being whipped in public.

Just as children could be sentenced to a few days' hard labour and a whipping during the nineteenth century, adults too were sometimes given a custodial sentence together with corporal punishment. John Davis, a weaver from Wotton-under-Edge, was convicted of stealing a piece of cashmere cloth from Samuel and William Long in 1829.[7] Aged around thirty-three at the time, John, a poor man supporting his wife and children, had probably stolen out of economic need, aiming to sell the cloth on. He was sentenced to three months' hard labour in the Horsley House of Correction, together with a public whipping.

After his incarceration, John, like many others in his situation – poor and therefore unable to migrate to a different area – had to return to his home and live amongst his neighbours, many of whom would have known of, or witnessed, his punishment. But this public embarrassment didn't seem to affect his employment prospects; in the 1841, 1851 and 1861 censuses for Wotton-under-Edge, John is still listed as being employed as a cloth weaver.

In the late eighteenth century, and turn of the nineteenth century, whipping was an infrequent punishment in the Cotswolds, if the surviving Calendars of Prisoners are anything to go by. However, where whipping was specified as a punishment, it was age-blind, with both children and adults being sentenced. In 1800, for example, two males were sentenced to imprisonment and whipping. One was twelve-year-old Thomas Hinton from Gloucestershire, although the records of his arrest are missing so it is unclear whereabouts in the county he was from. He was convicted of stealing bacon, cheese and money, and sentenced to two years in prison and to be 'privately whipped at the end of the first fortnight and of every succeeding three months of the said term.'[8]

A month after Thomas' conviction, thirty-six-year-old Charles Webb was charged with having broken into the house of Charles Evans in Highgrove, near Tetbury, and stolen a quantity of bacon. In March 1801, he was tried and found guilty. Although he received a more lenient jail term than Thomas Hinton – six months – he was ordered to pay a fine of one shilling and to be publicly whipped.[9]

Thomas Davis, thirty-four, was convicted of assaulting two children in 1818 and sentenced to two-and-a-half years in the Northleach House of Correction, together with a whipping. He was joined in the prison by John Baglin, forty-two, convicted of grand larceny and given two years at Northleach and a whipping.[10]

Around the end of 1822, whipping unofficially stopped at Northleach for a while. This was partly because fines were becoming a more popular form of punishment in the area – fines became common for those convicted of disobeying an order of bastardy, for example. But in 1830 the whippings resumed, with at least three cases of the punishment being doled out at Northleach over the next year. Eleven-year-old Joseph Moss was sentenced to a week in prison and a whipping after stealing a silver spoon in Lower

Lower Swell's Joseph Moss was whipped, aged eleven.

Swell in September 1830;[11] thirteen-year-old William Wells was twice whipped during his twelve-month prison sentence for stealing a gown; and sixteen-year-old Thomas Bush was whipped three times during his twelve-month sentence for larceny.[12]

While the break in whippings was restricted to Northleach; the punishment continued to be carried out at the main penitentiary at Gloucester both during Northleach's break, and after. In 1832, nineteen-year-old Charles White was convicted of stealing a pair of corduroy trousers from John Waldron in Stow-on-the-Wold (hopefully while John wasn't wearing them!) and sentenced to eight months in the penitentiary and one whipping.[13]

Whipping itself was broken down into three separate punishments: private whipping, whipping in front of other prisoners, and a public whipping.

Sixteen-year-old James Davis had to undergo a whipping 'in front of the prisoners' at Gloucester Gaol in 1819, after being convicted of stealing a rabbit, whereas Thomas Carpenter, also sixteen, had been sentenced to a private whipping six years earlier.[14]

Whether whipping encouraged children or teenage boys to subsequently keep to the straight and narrow is unclear; but it is evident that it didn't always serve as a learning experience. For example, twelve-year-old Daniel Whymans, an apprentice, was convicted in 1816 of 'frequently running away' from his employer. He was given three months in Little Dean House of Correction, and ordered to be privately whipped on four different occasions. Two years later, the now fourteen-year-old boy was again in court, charged with leaving his master's service. This time, he was given three months in the House of Correction and ordered to be whipped three times.[15] Presumably the boy's dislike of his trade or his employer was more than his fear of being whipped.

A public whipping in a local House of Correction may have been slightly more tolerable – or less humiliating – than at the main gaol in Gloucester. The Northleach House of Correction, standing on the edge of town, just outside the village of Hampnett, was fairly small, and on occasion might have only had a couple of dozen prisoners being held there. But, conversely, the severity of the whipping itself may have been dependent on the person wielding the birch; there may not have been much uniformity in how the punishment was delivered from place to place.

Some people were ordered to be whipped because of their economic status. Henry VIII's Whipping Act permitted vagrants to be carried on the back of carts through towns, whilst being whipped. The Cheltenham Manor Court Rolls record a new whipping post being set up in Arle, just west of Cheltenham, in 1630, in order to 'punish rogues and vagrants'.[16] Five years before weaver John Davis was publicly whipped, the 1824 Vagrancy Act had been passed, stating that vagrants could be punished by being whipped before being returned to their place of settlement. The Act, brought in during George IV's reign, was in part created to deal with the number of soldiers who had fought in the Napoleonic Wars, and who had returned to unemployment and homelessness. Their economic plight was made worse by the increasing numbers of migrants both from other parts of the UK – mainly Scotland and Ireland – and elsewhere, seeking work in England. Section 10 of the Act made it an offence to sleep on the streets or to beg, and also enabled judges to sentence 'rogues and vagabonds and incorrigible rogues' found guilty under the Act to hard labour and whipping.[17] Needless to say, all vagrants were classified as being 'idle and disorderly persons, rogues and vagabonds'.

Prior to the Vagrancy Act, beggars and the homeless in the Cotswolds had been examined by the authorities and issued with vagrants' passes to transfer them back to their legal place of settlement. Their passes would be checked at each parish or place they stopped en route, and food and lodging provided for them by the local churchwardens or similar. Although they were usually classified on their passes as being rogues and vagabonds, this was more a turn of phrase designed to justify moving them out of an area. The poor cost parishes money, and so they were keen to move them back to the area where they had previously worked or lived.

In 1747, for example, William Strange was apprehended by one Benjamin Baker in the city of Gloucester, after Baker saw Strange begging on the streets. He took him before the city mayor, Gabriel Harris JP, who examined Strange. He found that this vagrant was:

> … about 50 years of age, by trade a glover, and that the place of his legal settlement is at the parish of Cirencester in the county of Gloucester where he received his apprenticeship to one John Fitchons, and that he hath done no act since whereby to gain any other legal settlement.[18]

The master of the local House of Correction, where Strange had initially been sent, was ordered to convey the glover to the constable at Kingsholm – the first place he would need to pass through in order to get back to Cirencester. The constable would check his settlement pass, and then transport him to the next parish, and so on, until he reached his place of legal settlement.

There were some sad cases, such as Hester Lawton, found begging with her eight-year-old daughter Ethel in Gloucester in 1752. Hester was married to a soldier who was away fighting, leaving his wife and child to fend for themselves. Regardless of their circumstances, Hester and her daughter were sent back to Sudeley, where Hester had previously lived with her husband, to cope as best as they could.[19]

Another case was Elizabeth Markham of Finmere, in Oxfordshire, who was found begging in Cirencester in October 1764. She had been in service in her home village, but her job had ended after a year, and for the past two months she had been on the streets, selling anything she could in order to get

Elizabeth Markham was found begging here in Cirencester.

food. She now had nothing left to sell and was reduced to complete poverty. After being examined by the Justice of the Peace in Cirencester, she was ordered back to Finmere, reporting to the constable for Burford en route.[20]

It may seem harsh to modern eyes to send these poverty-stricken men, women and children back to parishes that, in some cases, they hadn't lived in for some time. However, there was little of the public humiliation seen through whipping the 'undeserving poor' – as they became regarded – during the nineteenth century; Georgian vagrants in the region seem to have been treated with a bit more kindness and understanding, despite the British History website stating that in the 1760s, a person seen as idle and disorderly

Ready to whip. (© Carolyn Ford, and used with permission)

was liable to receive a whipping from the north gate of Gloucester Prison, round the market, and to Southgate Street.[21] However, the records from this time do not contain any evidence of a vagrant being treated in this way.

The length of a whipping varied according to the crime. Someone found guilty of obtaining money by false pretences, for example, might be whipped along the whole length of Gloucester's Westgate Street and back.[22]

In 1871, Finlay Dunn – a forty-year-old land agent living in Long Compton – gave a talk to the Banbury Chamber of Agriculture regarding vagrancy. He quoted talks he had had with Gloucestershire's Chief Constable, Henry Christian, where the latter had differentiated between vagrants who walked 12 to 15 miles a day, and those who were merely 'loitering' and only covering a third of the distance. The latter were made to do unpaid work before being made to leave the local poor law union. Dunn's own view of this was:

> When such determined vagrants are caught offending against the Vagrant Act [*sic*] or otherwise, I do not see why their punishment should not be more severe than heretofore, why during a somewhat longer imprisonment they should not at intervals, if able-bodied males, be treated to occasional whipping.[23]

Dunn described vagrants as being like a lower species of animal, who have to be whipped to stimulate them, and stop them being 'dullards'. One suspects that his scathing attitude towards vagrants, and his view of them as animals rather than humans, was not an isolated view.

Attitudes towards whipping changed over time. In May 1800, William Crump of Tewkesbury was convicted of twice leaving his family chargeable to the parish, and was sentenced to be publicly whipped in Tewkesbury's market place. The *Gloucester Journal* noted, 'Had it not been for the lenity of the magistrates, he might have been transported for seven years.'[24]

At this point, whipping was seen as a more lenient punishment than being transported, but when the Seduction Laws Amendment Bill of 1873 was being debated in Parliament, MPs queried whether whipping was a suitable punishment for those convicted of sexual assault on a girl under twelve. Some argued that the punishment was not 'desirable' because it contained 'a principle of vindictive punishment'. However, others argued in favour, as it would be 'calculated to have a more deterrent effect than mere imprisonment'. This whipping clause was approved by a majority of MPs.[25]

Whipping, both for boys and adults, was only abolished in 1948.

## Notes

[1] *Morning Post*, London, 23 October 1848, p. 2

[2] *Jackson's Oxford Journal*, 19 October 1861

[3] *Berrow's Worcester Journal*, 6 September 1862

[4] National Archives reference PCOM 2/290/79, dated 11/1/1873

[5] National Archives reference PCOM 2/290/164

[6] National Archives reference HO 44/21

[7] Gloucestershire Archives reference G/49/A/27

[8] Calendar of Prisoners, Gloucestershire Archives reference Q/SG/2/1800

[9] Calendar of Prisoners, Gloucestershire Archives reference Q/SG/2/1801

[10] Calendar of Prisoners, Gloucestershire Archives reference Q/SG/2/1818

[11] Calendar of Prisoners, Gloucestershire Archives reference Q/SG/2/1830

[12] Calendar of Prisoners, Gloucestershire Archives reference Q/SG/2/1831

[13] Calendar of Prisoners, Gloucestershire Archives reference Q/SG/2/1832

[14] Calendar of Prisoners, Gloucestershire Archives reference Q/SG/1/1819

[15] Calendar of Prisoners, Gloucestershire Archives reference Q/SG/1/1816 and Q/SG/1/1818

[16] 'The History of Hesters Way', by Chris Green, accessed via http://www.bubbleserver.co.uk/hwnp/history/vol2/hhw2_3.php

[17] www.statutelaw.gov.uk/content.aspx?activeTextDocid-1029462

[18] Vagrants' settlement passes, Gloucestershire Archives reference Q/Rv/1/9

[19] Vagrants' settlement passes, Gloucestershire Archives reference Q/Rv/1

[20] Vagrants' settlement passes, Gloucestershire Archives reference Q/Rv/2

[21] 'Gloucester, 1720-1835: City Government' in NM Herbert (ed) (1988), pp 141-152, accessed via www.british-history.ac.uk/report.aspx?compid=42293

22 'Gloucester, 1720-1835: City Government' in NM Herbert (ed) (1988), pp 141-152, accessed via www.british-history.ac.uk/report. aspx?compid=42293

23 *Jackson's Oxford Journal*, 1 April 1871

24 *Gloucester Journal*, 5 May 1800

25 *The Times*, 8 July 1873, p. 6

# 7

# THE PILLORY

The pillory, or whipping post, was a form of punishment aimed at humiliating those convicted of crimes that were seen as the worst outside of those resulting in a death sentence. It consisted of a wooden frame, mounted on a post. The convicted person would be trapped, either by head or limbs, into holes or rings within this frame. Related to the stocks, of which the Cotswolds had quite a few, it has been used as a punishment since at least the twelfth century. By the early nineteenth century, 'pillory' had become another word for humiliation or ridicule, but an early nineteenth-century edition of the *Morning Post* referred to its use as a means of torture, when it detailed the case of a Catholic bookseller in Oxford, Roland Jinks, who was convicted of selling religious material in 1577 and sentenced to 'have both his ears nailed to the pillory, and to deliver himself by cutting them off with his own hands.'[1]

As the pillory was used for more serious crimes than the stocks, and was perceived as being for 'bad' men, onlookers and passers-by tended to be more aggressive towards those in the pillory and would often throw things at them. When stones were thrown, serious injury, or in some cases death, could result.

The intention was to embarrass the criminal, and so pillories were made as visible as possible, and erected at times and on days that were likely to be busy – such as market days, when public places would be full of people to watch the convicted suffer. In 1839, the *Oxford Journal* referred to some politicians as looking 'deadly pale, crestfallen and woebegone, more like culprits in the pillory than Ministers of State',[2] illustrating the contemporary view that being sentenced to the pillory would be a shock to the system of criminals and encourage them to seek a quieter, law-abiding life.

The use of the pillory as a source of public humiliation can be seen in the use of the pillory as a punishment for those convicted in the eighteenth century for what were termed 'unnatural' crimes, such as homosexuality and bestiality.

The *Gloucester Journal* eagerly covered a case in December 1730 where William Hollowell, a beadle with the Sadler's Company, was convicted of attempting to commit an act of sodomy on William Huggins, a waterman, in St Paul's churchyard in London. Huggins was convicted of 'permitting it'. Both were handed down fines, a prison sentence, and also made to stand in the pillory in the churchyard. They were convicted on 15 December; on 29 December, the *Gloucester Journal* breathlessly stated:

> They were severely handled by the Populace, who tore their Cloaths off their Backs, and then whipt them severely, and pelted them with mud, rotten eggs, etc. They were taken down 25 minutes before their Time was expired, on account they were judg'd to be expiring.[3]

It is evident that such punishments were designed not only to punish the convicted, but also to act as a warning to others not to commit the same offence. The embarrassment or humiliation of being in the pillory should have been enough; but added to this Hollowell and Huggins had to undergo whipping and throwing of missiles by the public that nearly amounted to a public execution. In addition, their case made the papers as far away

A man in the pillory. (© Carolyn Ford, and used with permission)

as Gloucestershire, with theirs serving as a salutary tale to others across the country.

Closer to home, in 1778, one Francis Proctor was convicted at the Summer Assizes in Gloucester of bestiality, and ordered to be imprisoned for two years 'and in the meantime to stand in the Pillory three times.'[4] Proctor was then ordered to be enlisted in the army and was signed up to the 9th Regiment.

Although the Gloucester Castle prison records don't record the exact nature of Proctor's crime, it was obviously seen as bad; in the Cotswolds in the eighteenth and nineteenth centuries, many rural lads were convicted of bestiality. For someone discovering his sexual urges, in the absence of amenable women, there were always animals around, and cases record example of 'unnatural behaviour' with sheep, horses and even cows. But not many of these cases were punished with the pillory, which does make one wonder what exactly Proctor was discovered to be doing.

Both men and women could be pilloried, and sometimes the punishment was carried out very quickly, in order to accommodate a subsequent punishment. For example, on 18 July 1752, Joan Reade was found guilty of perjury, and sentenced to be transported. However, she was also ordered to be put in the pillory and this was carried out three days later. She was then returned to Gloucester Castle to await arrangements for her transportation to America.[5]

One of the most notorious cases in the Cotswolds occurred in 1796, when twenty-seven-year-old Kid Wake was arrested for what was termed a 'high misdemeanour' against the king, George III. According to the Newgate Calendar, on 29 October 1795, the king had been in his coach, making his way to Parliament, when a group of people, including Kid, started hissing and yelling out, 'No war! Down with him!' The group grew rowdy, and were able to smash a window of the carriage before the king and his party escaped.

When Kid's case went to trial at the court of the King's Bench on 7 May 1796, much was made of Kid's 'contorted countenance'. It was common to prejudge someone's guilt on the basis of their looks; conversely, Kid had no defence lawyer, as the court of the day assumed a man was innocent and that he needed no defence – instead, it was the job of the prosecution to prove a man's guilt. Kid argued that his suspect looks were actually due to a defect in his vision, which made him screw his eyes up when trying to focus on anything. However, the prosecution said this would not account for his bad language against George III.

Kid was sentenced to five years in the Gloucester Penitentiary with hard labour. However, this was only half his punishment; the Gloucestershire

Calendar of Prisoners adds that during his imprisonment, another punishment was to be carried out:

> ... in the course of the three first months of which [he was imprisoned], he is to stand an hour in the pillory in a public street of the City of Gloucester, on a market-day of the same city; and at the expiration of the said five years' imprisonment, he is to give his own security in the sum of 1,000l for his good behaviour, for the space of ten years, to commence from and after the expiration of the said term of five years ...[6]

If Kid failed to maintain his good behaviour during the ten years, he would be returned to prison.

The court saw this as a soft punishment, saying that Kid should have been 'convicted of a crime of a much higher nature' had those who had prosecuted him not been merciful.[7] This presumably means that he could have been charged with treason against the king and condemned to death.

But the court wanted to make an example of Kid, and so he was made to be exhibited in the pillory in the main city serving the Cotswolds, on its busiest day of the week, each week, so that the maximum number of people would observe him.

Gloucester's Westgate Street was the location of one of the town's pillories.

What Kid's family made of this humiliation is not clear. Kid, a literate man, was presumably from Gloucestershire originally, hence his punishment there, but he had been living in London before his arrest. He had married at St James, Clerkenwell, on 4 February 1793, and his wife, Charlotte Mary Storer, was in London while her husband was being humiliated in Gloucester.

Kid Wake received a punishment of the pillory for shouting at the king; another man received the same punishment for an altogether different crime.

John Moutry was arrested in September 1804, charged with assaulting an eleven-year-old girl, Elizabeth Bennett, and trying to rape her. The thirty-eight-year-old was tried on 2 October 1804 and found guilty of assault. He was given two years' imprisonment, and on the day of his release, was ordered to be put in the pillory near to Lawford's Gate Bridewell in Gloucester 'between the hours of twelve and two, for the space of one hour, and be then discharged.'[8]

It is clear that in the late eighteenth and early nineteenth centuries, the pillory was reserved for a few particular cases where it was felt that the public should be shown the consequences of acting in a particularly anti-social way. It was certainly only used in a few isolated cases in the Cotswolds. After John Moutry's turn on the pillory, it was a decade before the next case. In May 1813, thirty-year-old Benjamin Evans was charged with 'pretending, from his skill and knowledge in occult or crafty science, to discover where, or in what manner, some money, goods and chattels, which were supposed to have been stolen, might be found.'[9]

Britain had been suspicious of any activity that could be seen as witchcraft for centuries – and although the burning of 'witches' had long since ended, there was still a lack of understanding about any unexplainable behaviour and a desire to equate it with the occult. This fear of the unknown resulted in hasty arrests and over-the-top punishments. Evans was found guilty in July 1814 of his 'misdemeanour' and his punishment was:

> … to be imprisoned one year, and once in every quarter of the said year, at the Market Town of Stroud, on the last Friday in each quarter of the said year, being the market-day there, to stand on the pillory for the space of one hour.[10]

The local papers eagerly reported the rare instances of people being sentenced to the pillory. *Jackson's Oxford Journal* not only covered the cases of those who were pilloried in the centre of Oxford, but also those sentenced in neighbouring counties. This was partly because of the nature of the assizes, with judges touring round areas. If a group of judges had been known to have sentenced people to the pillory on neighbouring assizes, they might be likely to do the same when they reached Oxford.

In 1806, the *Oxford Journal* covered the case of Michael Crockett, who was found guilty of fraud at the Worcester Assizes, and sentenced to two years' imprisonment and to stand in the pillory at Bromsgrove the following Tuesday. After the details of the cases were heard at Worcester, it was noted: 'Their Lordships on leaving Worcester proceeded for Gloucestershire, where there are 11 prisoners for trial.'[11]

It was probably for a similar reason that the *Oxford Journal* covered the case of William Baynham, convicted of assaulting twelve-year-old Ann Braig at the Hereford Assizes and sentenced to six months in prison and one hour on the pillory[12] and the case of William Reynolds, convicted of assaulting Hannah Brown with intent to rape at the Worcester Assizes, and sentenced to be put on the pillory at Tenbury.[13] Other pillory cases from Birmingham and Warwick were also reported.

There were Oxfordshire cases, too. In 1800, John Tubb was sentenced to twelve months in prison and an hour in the pillory in the market place in Oxford, on market day, after being convicted of perjury - he had robbed banknotes from an Oxford bargemaster.[14]

In 1819, the *Oxford Journal* reported how, when one William Key was sentenced to stand in the Covent Garden pillory, a 'vast' number of onlookers threw rotten eggs, apples and mud at him so that 'long before the expiration of the hour he was so completely covered that his person was scarcely discernable'.[15]

Yet the pillory was seen as a suitable – indeed, sometimes a lenient – punishment by some. A correspondent to the *Oxford Journal* in 1826 asked for the reinstatement of a law from Edward VI's time that specified:

> If any bakers shall conspire not to sell their bread but at certain prices, every such person shall forfeit for the first offence 10l to the King, and if not paid in six days, he shall suffer 20 days' imprisonment, and shall only have bread and water for his sustenance; for the second offence, 40l a year, a pillory, and the loss of an ear, and to be taken as a man infamous and not to be credited.[16]

This correspondent thought such an act in nineteenth-century society would 'confer a benefit on the community'.

Some twenty years after Kid Wake was sentenced to the pillory, the punishment was still being used to make an example of otherwise unexplainable behaviour, but after 1816, its use was restricted, meaning that

Spectators would throw rotten vegetables at pilloried men - and note the cat being swung!

Oxford's Market Street – John Tubb stood in the pillory near here.

only those convicted of perjury or subornation were liable to be sentenced to it. It was formally abolished as a punishment in 1837, although the last recorded use of it in Britain was seven years earlier. D.N. Donaldson believes the Winchcombe borough whipping post was still present outside the Town Hall in 1800, but had been removed by 1839.[17]

By the end of the nineteenth century, the pillory was seen as an historic punishment, and one that filled the nostalgia slot of newspapers. In 1899, for example, a feature on the Neath stocks and pillory in South Wales caused readers to write into the *Western Mail* with their memories of the stocks' 'three pairs of leg-holes graduated in size'.

One elderly man wrote to the newspaper about his memories of the pillory. He said that as a young boy, he had got hold of a 'greenhorn' and fixed him into the pillory; and he referred to having an ancient 1713 copy of leet court punishments that included the pillory.[18] At this point in time, it was only the elderly who could remember the pillory being in use within their lifetime; soon, nobody was left who could remember the pillory being used.

## Notes

[1] *Morning Post*, 5 November 1835

[2] *Oxford Journal*, 16 November 1839

[3] *Gloucester Journal*, 29 December 1730

[4] Calendar of Prisoners, Gloucestershire Archives reference Q/SG1 (1771-1779)

[5] *Gloucester Journal*, 21 July 1753

[6] Calendar of Prisoners, Gloucestershire Archives reference Q/SG1/1795

[7] The Newgate Calendar, accessed via http://www.exclassics.com/newgate/ng388.htm

[8] Calendar of Prisoners, Gloucestershire Archives reference Q/SG/2/1804

[9] Calendar of Prisoners, Gloucestershire Archives reference Q/SG2/1814

[10] Calendar of Prisoners, Gloucestershire Archives reference Q/SG/2/1814

[11] *Jackson's Oxford Journal*, 2 August 1806

[12] *Jackson's Oxford Journal*, 28 March 1807

[13] *Jackson's Oxford Journal*, 27 August 1808

[14] *Jackson's Oxford Journal*, 8 March 1800

[15] *Jackson's Oxford Journal*, 2 January 1819

[16] *Jackson's Oxford Journal*, 25 February 1826

[17] Donaldson, D.N. (2002), p. 131

[18] *Western Mail*, 14 July 1893

# 8

# THE STOCKS

On the far side of Market Square in Stow-on-the-Wold is a set of stocks, which have stood there for the past 500 years.

The phrase 'the stocks' is an abbreviation of stockade; wooden boards into which people's feet would be locked in place. They were designed in the medieval era both for punishment and public humiliation, making people sit in a public place – often a market place such as in Stow – to be assaulted at whim. Ostensibly, those put in them were supposed to learn from the experience, and emerge a reformed character – in *King Lear*, Kent regards the stocks as a waste in his case, because he is too mature and set in his ways to reform: 'Sir, I am too old to learn: call not your stocks for me.'[1]

The public humiliation afforded by the stocks was permitted as those who were placed in them were criminals – often convicted of minor crimes, but who were seen to have offended the standard modes of conduct.

However, although minor crimes could result in a stay in the stocks, the punishment could sometimes equate to a death sentence. People were put in the stocks in all weathers, sometimes staying there day and night. This sometimes led to convicted men and women dying of heat exhaustion or, conversely, hypothermia, as a result of their punishment in the open air.

The public eagerly tormented those unfortunate enough to be placed in the stocks – throwing their rubbish at them, tickling them, or even whipping their uncovered, and restricted, feet.

The Stow-on-the-Wold stocks.

Crimes that could be punished with a spell in the stocks – with either ankles, hands or head placed in the holes in the boards – included military desertion. Criminals had to rely on friends to bring them anything more substantial than bread and water for sustenance.

Most parishes seem to have had their own set of stocks. In Gloucester city, there were a pillory and stocks in Southgate Street that were still being occasionally used for petty criminals in the early nineteenth century, until imprisonment in Gloucester Gaol replaced it as the usual punishment. A further set of stocks existed at the bottom of Burford Road in Chipping Norton, but these seem to have been removed by the mid-nineteenth century. Chipping Norton's Oxfordshire neighbours, Burford, Banbury, Watlington and Abingdon, also had their own stocks up until the 1840s.

The stocks were often listed as an alternative punishment to fines; if they did not pay up within a certain period of time, such as one week, they had to endure a few hours in their local stocks instead. Policemen were also known to use the threat of the stocks to make errant schoolboys behave. The stocks were either situated in a market place, or near the local lock-up, as was the case at Cirencester. Some stocks are still preserved in churchyards – such as the set at Forthampton, near Tewkesbury, which are next to a whipping post with manacles, and could hold three people at a time[2] – but this may not have been their original location.

In 1823, Robert Peel, as Home Secretary, introduced the Gaol Act, which stopped whipping, expulsion and the stocks being used as punishments for 'idle and disorderly persons'. The punishment had decreased for other crimes by the start of Victoria's reign, although in October 1839, Thomas Smith was put into the stocks at Burford for six hours after failing to pay the 10 shillings he had previously been fined for being drunk and disorderly.[3]

The stocks were regularly used in Oxfordshire and Gloucestershire as an alternative punishment where people had been handed down a fine as an original sentence, but had been unable to pay it. However, this led to some magistrates trying to make petty criminals serve time in the stocks when they refused to pay a fine, which led to the Queen's Bench having to discuss the issue in February 1849.

This followed the case of a Robert Barton in Oxford, who had been convicted of selling fruit on a Sunday, and fined five shillings, with an additional eleven shillings in costs. When he failed to pay, an Oxford Justice of the Peace ordered that Barton be put in the stocks for two hours. Barton appointed a solicitor to try and quash the conviction, who argued that magistrates had no jurisdiction to put someone in the stocks for failing to pay the costs associated with their case. Instead, argued the solicitor, if Barton failed to pay the costs, he should be sent to a house of correction or county gaol instead – he could only legally be put in the stocks for failing to pay the initial fine, which he had, in fact, paid. The Queen's Court agreed that the relevant statute did not cover the imposition of the stocks

Stocks used to exist here on Gloucester's Southgate Street.

The bottom of Burford Road, Chipping Norton. Stocks once stood here.

as a means of recovering a financial penalty, and quashed the conviction – a warning to other courts and magistrates to be careful about when to use the stocks.[4]

By the 1840s, many stocks had fallen into disrepair. Although Richard Muir, in his *Landscape Encyclopaedia*, states that 'a remarkable number of village stocks survive, and this must reflect the fact that this rough and ready form of punishment by public humiliation endured until the start of Victorian times',[5] the punishment in fact continued some years after Victoria became Queen; although when it was given as a sentence, it could cause some problems for towns that had failed to maintain their old stocks.

In 1859, for example, *Jackson's Oxford Journal* noted 'considerable excitement' in Chipping Norton, after a young man was sentenced to be confined in the borough's stocks. George Bartlett, the man in question, had been convicted of being drunk and disorderly, and had been fined. As was common in Oxfordshire and Gloucestershire up to the 1830s, when someone was unable to pay their fine they were given an alternative punishment, such as imprisonment or a spell in the stocks. Bartlett, a twenty-year-old

Cirencester's stocks were once outside the town lock-up, pictured here.

Middle Row, Chipping
Norton, the home of
George Bartlett.

hairdresser living with his family on the town's Middle Row, hadn't got the
means of paying his fine, and so was ordered to go in the stocks.

However, the *Journal* reported that it was some years since the stocks
had been used in the town – and that, in fact, these stocks had actually
decayed because they had stood idle for so long. As a result, George Bartlett's
punishment had to be deferred for a week until the Oxfordshire County
portable stocks were located and transferred to Chipping Norton.

In the meantime, Bartlett had become, understandably, worried about the
punishment, and the prospect of being humiliated in front of his neighbours.
He managed to escape from the town's police station, and hid out elsewhere
in the town.

Unfortunately for him, though, he boasted of his escape, and rather than
hiding indoors or making his way to another town where he wasn't known,
he was spotted wandering around Chipping Norton by Inspector Thorogood
of the station from which he had absconded. The inspector told Bartlett that
he was wanted at the station 'for a short time', and when the gullible Bartlett

Winchcombe Town Hall.

The Winchcombe stocks.

followed him there, he was immediately put into the stocks, where he remained for the next six hours, 'an object of attraction to a great many persons'.[6]

This may not have been the last use of the stocks in the Cotswolds; the Cirencester stocks, near The Shambles, were only used prior to 1859,[7] but there may have been a case in Winchcombe in 1860 of a man put in the stocks, which were outside the Town Hall, for being drunk.[8]

The last recorded use of the stocks in Britain was in Wales in 1872. By this time, stocks were seen as a historical curiosity, a remnant of an archaic system, with towns seeking to preserve them as museum exhibits or a tourist attraction. By 1887, the Winchcombe parish stocks had been in the Sudeley Castle Museum for some time, when local resident J.H. Stephens, supported by the local vicar, Robert Noble Jackson, suggested that they should be returned to their previous position outside the Town Hall.

There were veiled accusations that Sudeley Castle had 'stolen' the town's property to create a focal point of their museum, which led to the Castle's Emma Dent telling the *Evesham Journal* that the stocks had been neglected by the townspeople and had been taken to her home for safekeeping, with the permission of Winchcombe town sheriff Dr Thomas Newman. The *Journal* reported that the castle was willing to return the stocks immediately to the town, where they still stand in their original position outside the Town Hall, an attraction today just as they were a century ago.[9]

## Notes

[1] *King Lear*, Act 2, Scene 2, 130
[2] British Listed Buildings, accessed via http://www.britishlistedbuildings. co.uk/en-134184-stocks-and-whipping-post-circa-35-metres
[3] *Jackson's Oxford Journal*, 5 October 1839
[4] *Jackson's Oxford Journal*, 17 February 1849
[5] Richard Muir (2004), page 240
[6] *Jackson's Oxford Journal*, 15 October 1859
[7] Timothy Darvill and Christopher Gerrard (1994), page 129
[8] D.N. Donaldson (2001), page 131
[9] D.N. Donaldson (2001), pp 188–189

# 9

# THE DUCKING STOOL

The ducking stool – and its close equivalents, the cucking stool and the tumbrel – was, like the stocks, pillory and whipping post, designed to humiliate errant locals by punishing them in a public arena.

The oldest type of stool was, in fact, the cucking stool, which had probably existed since Anglo-Saxon times. A wooden chair placed on poles, it was used more commonly from the sixteenth century, and up to the mid-eighteenth century to embarrass initially fraudulent tradesmen and later, scolds. Unlike the ducking stool – where the chair was attached to a pole which was used to dip the chair and occupant into water – the cucking stool didn't traditionally involve water (although its name is often interchangeable with the ducking stool), but was, instead, lifted into the air so that the maximum number of spectators could get a clear view of the person being 'cucked'. Alternatively, the cucking stool might be wheeled around a town to ensure that everyone got a good look at the scold, or a chance to throw things at her if they had taken against her.

Women being ducked were placed in the ducking stool and either tied there with chains or with an iron belt round their middle. The chairs were often made of oak, and were hefty contraptions. But at least the ducking stools involved only a brief immersion into water; the tumbrel, a chair on two wheels that was pushed into a pond, tipping the occupant backwards into the water, could more frequently kill their victims.

There were numerous ducking stools in Gloucestershire until the eighteenth century, after which they fell out of use. They weren't present everywhere – in the mid-seventeenth century, the inhabitants of Stonehouse, near Stroud, proudly declaimed that 'wee have neyther pillory, whipping post nor Gumstole [*sic*] for the punishment of Roagues and offenders';[1] but there was certainly one in Bristol, for example, known to exist as far back as the sixteenth century; it was also apparently used for the last time on one Mistress Blake – who had been scolding her husband – in 1718. Unfortunately for the town's mayor, Edmund Mountjoy, who had ordered the punishment, Mistress Blake's husband subsequently charged him with battery, humiliating the mayor and putting him off sentencing anyone else to be ducked.[2]

In the Cotswolds, a ducking stool was used in a pond known as the horsepool, at the bottom of Gumstool Hill in Tetbury – gumstool being the local word for a ducking stool, and possibly originating in the word 'gummy', meaning 'mouthy' or to speak rudely. In the thirteenth century, Gumstool Hill was known as Cirencester Street and was the main route through Tetbury, being on the main Bristol to Cirencester road. A ducking here would have been visible to many, and act as a deterrent to others. It is believed that the Tetbury ducking stool was being used from the fifteenth century, with the first recorded use being in 1502.[3]

A ducking stool. (© Carolyn Ford, and used with permission)

Tetbury's ducking pond was once here, on Gumstool Hill.

The Tetbury gumstool caused the local men charged with building and maintaining it a lot of grief. In 1656, according to local historian Eric Hodgson, the parish overseers were reprimanded for not having a cucking stool, despite a statute specifying that they should, and a year later, they were saying that they needed more time to obtain both a cucking stool and pillory.[4] Even once made and in place, they were liable to damage or wear and tear. In 1660, the parish constables were censured for not having kept the pillory and cucking stool in good repair, and in the late eighteenth century, both the town stocks and whipping post needed repairs.[5]

There was also a ducking stool at Winyard Street in Winchcombe. Originally known as Vineyard Street, it was part of Winchcombe Abbey's vineyard. However, at one point, it changed its name to Duck Street, after an eighteenth-century ducking stool at the riverside on the River Isbourne here. When excavations for a new bridge on the street were carried out, a stump, believed to be from the old ducking stool, was uncovered.[6]

In the neighbouring counties of Worcestershire and Herefordshire, other gumstools existed; in Upton-upon-Severn, Goom Stool Cottages, which existed from the 1400s until they were demolished in 1882, were built near

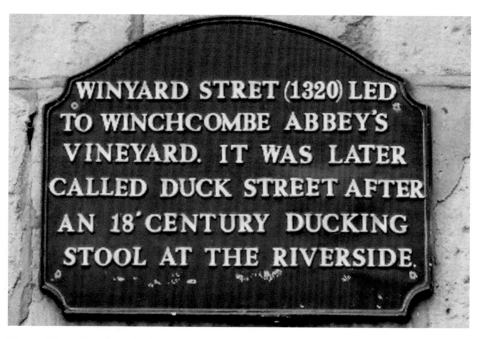

WINYARD STRET (1320) LED TO WINCHCOMBE ABBEY'S VINEYARD. IT WAS LATER CALLED DUCK STREET AFTER AN 18´ CENTURY DUCKING STOOL AT THE RIVERSIDE.

Vineyard Street, Winchcombe, formerly Duck Street.

Today's idyllic view down Winchcombe's Vineyard Street is at odds with its grim history.

the town's ducking pool.[7] In Leominster, the Priory still contains the ducking stool that was used for centuries in this part of Herefordshire. Leominster was also the hometown of the last woman known to have been tied to the ducking stool – Sarah Leeke, who was supposed to undergo the punishment in 1817, only the water level in the ducking pond was too low, and she ended up being simply wheeled round the town instead.[8]

Other related punishments, aimed specifically at women, existed alongside the ducking stool. The scold-cart was used to publicly humiliate women convicted of being scolds (the crime of being a 'common scold' – disturbing the peace of one's neighbourhood by constant scolding or the use of abusive language, according to the Oxford English Dictionary – has existed since at least the late fifteenth century, and by the eighteenth century only applied to women under law). The first recorded use of the scold-cart was in Nottingham in 1569, but there is little evidence for this vehicle being used in the Cotswolds. By 1858, it was included in a book on obsolete punishments.[9]

In 1879, the common law crime of being a 'common scold' was abolished under a new criminal code. When *The Times* covered the proposed abolition, it noted that the general public were, by this time, 'ignorant' that being a scold was a crime – it had obviously fallen into disuse as a charge by this point.

*The Times* also noted that the crime was seen as a specifically female one, whereby women were perceived as being 'a nuisance to the neighbourhood' by scolding. A woman could be convicted even though it was not necessary to give any examples of her expressions in evidence. *The Times* noted:

> The punishment provided for the offence is peculiar. The scold is placed in 'a certain engine of correction called the tre-bucket or cucking stool,' which, says Coke (3 Inst. 219), 'in law signifieth a stool that falleth down into a pit of water for the punishment of the party in it'.[10]

Although it may seem surprising that such a medieval-sounding punishment may have still existed in the statute books until this fairly late date, it is worth emphasising that *The Times* not only had to explain the crime to its readers, but also what a ducking stool was.

By the turn of the twentieth century, such things as the ducking stool – or, as it was also known, the scold's chair – were remnants of an older, less humane society. In 1907, *The Times* recorded an auction of contents from a Hampshire manor house that included a scold's chair – 'a fine specimen of that ancient instrument of torture'. The chair, which dated from 1723, was made of oak and elaborately carved with kneeling figures and coats of arms, in a Gothic style. It was also inscribed with a poem:

> If you have a wife who scolds/Life indeed is bitter/So in this chair youed better sit her/Then go out to take your pleasure/Come back, release her at your leisure/And after all too light a measure.[11]

The newspaper noted that the scold's chair was commonly used up to and throughout the early eighteenth century, with a late case being recorded in Surrey in 1801. Apparently, the scold's chair, like, *The Times* drily noted, the parish pump, was funded out of the parish rates, and a scold's ducking in it was presented as a public ceremony. Although twentieth-century society saw itself as modern and humane, one wonders how many secretly agreed with Edward Walford, whose book *Greater London* was quoted in *The Times*:

> The ways of our ancestors were rough and ready, and one can but regret that the punishment has not been retained for those backbiters and slanderers who are the curse of the neighbourhood in which they live.[12]

Another punishment for women deemed to be scolds was the scold's bridle – like a horse's bridle, but designed to restrain women and, more specifically, their ability to talk, as well as to act as a public humiliation. In 1884, surviving bridles were recorded as being at Walsall, Chesterfield, Lichfield, Macclesfield and Ham Hall in Staffordshire. The vicar of Walton-on-Thames, in 1949, noted that his own local example had a well-worn bit – 'perhaps … bitten off by some dead and good virago'.[13] This bridle dated from 1632, and those punished would be chained to the church porch whilst wearing the bridle.

In 1949, *The Times* recorded the exhibition of what was, erroneously, thought to be the last surviving scold's bridle at the

Royal Agricultural Show at Shrewsbury.[14] These bridles were usually made of thin strips of iron, with holes for eyes, nose and upper lip. There was a platform that rested on the tongue which made it impossible for the wearer to remove it. The wearer would be padlocked into the device and be unable to speak whilst wearing it. A Warwickshire letter writer to *The Times* in 1949 remarked that the bridle had an advantage over the stocks, for:

> … with this contraption, the unfortunate lady might be left free, when wearing it, to carry on with her domestic duties, thus saving valuable time.[15]

## Notes

[1] 'List of constables and tithingmen in court rolls for Winterbotham family

of Stonehouse Court', court book 1632-1666, Gloucestershire Archives
   reference D445/M4

[2] 'A Chronological Outline of the History of Bristol', by John Evans (1824),
   accessed via http://www.rogerco.freeserve.co.uk/history/259.htm

[3] 'Tetbury: Growth of the Town and Outlying Settlements', from NM
   Herbert (ed.) (1976), pp 260-264, accessed via http://www.british-history.
   ac.uk/report.aspx?compid=19142

[4] Eric Hodgson (1976), p. 62

[5] Eric Hodgson (1976), p. 62

[6] Winchcombe Welcome Walkers, accessed via http://www.
   winchcombewelcomeswalkers.com/documents/Belas_Knap_walk.pdf

[7] The Ledbury Portal, accessed via http://www.ledburyportal.co.uk/portal/
   index.php?option=com_content&view=article&id=2352%3Acommon-
   scold-a-goomstool&catid=207%3Ahistory&Itemid=128

[8] Herefordshire Council, accessed via http://www.herefordshire.gov.uk/
   htt/759.aspx

[9] *Oxford English Dictionary*, accessed via www.oxfordshire.gov.uk/libraries

[10] *The Times*, Monday 28 April 1879, p. 8, quoting from the Solicitors' Journal

[11] *The Times*, 22 October 1907, p. 4

[12] *The Times*, 22 October 1907, p. 4

[13] *The Times*, 15 August 1949, p. 5

[14] *The Times*, 9 August 1949, p. 8

[15] *The Times*, 9 August 1949, p. 8

# 10

# WORKHOUSE PUNISHMENTS

After the 1834 Poor Law Amendment Act came into effect, there was a change in attitude towards the poor. Paupers were generally seen as being undeserving of help, and therefore, once admitted to a Cotswold workhouse, were expected to be obedient, dutiful, hardworking and well-behaved, and to be aware of how low down they were in the pecking order.

There was little appreciation on the part of the authorities that these were people whose dire financial straits had led them to be admitted into stark surroundings, separated from their families and made to work, in return for a hard bed and bland, small meals in return.

It is no wonder that many workhouse inhabitants rebelled. There are many instances of these 'able-bodied paupers' refusing to do the work set for them – usually the finger-hurting, mind-numbing task of oakum picking – or trying to climb the workhouse walls and abscond, or indulging in petty vandalism as a protest.

It was recognised that some workhouse inmates did not see why they should be put to work, often on pointless tasks such as picking oakum. Some workhouse masters employed physical force to make inmates work, or failing that, imprisonment. Even these punishments did not always work. A year after the General Order governing workhouse punishments was issued, Suffolk's Sir John Walsham was quoted as saying:

I yesterday inquired at Stow Union Workhouse about the disturbances which had lately taken place among the vagrants relieved in that establishment. It seems, they now make a point of refusing to work (the work at Stow workhouse consists in picking 1lb of oakum in four hours) and usually accompany such refusal by breaking the windows of their room, and burning the oakum in the fire supplied to them. For this misconduct they always assign as a reason the wish to lay up for a fortnight during the winter in gaol.[1]

Being in the workhouse was designed to punish the 'idle' poor, but even so, the workhouses were supposed to meet a basic standard of care. Yet there was no uniformity in how each Poor Law Union discharged its duties, and, according to which workhouse you found yourself in, the daily life there could be more of a punishment than if you were in another.

For example, in the 1830s, Cirencester Workhouse came under fire for the diet it gave its inmates. *The Times* pitied the 'destitute man in the workhouse of Cirencester [who] has the misfortune to possess as craving an appetite, and is compelled to toil as many hours, as the London Union pauper'.[2] Cirencester inmates received fifty-nine ounces of food less a week than their London counterparts, and seventeen pints of liquid less! In the London

Union Street, where the Stow Workhouse was located.

Union, inmates received twenty-six pints of 'liquids with vegetables' each week – Cirencester inmates received none.

All inmates received a standard diet in terms of the types of food they were allowed. The usual foodstuffs were basic – bread, gruel or porridge, potatoes, and occasionally meat. The Poor Law Boards stipulated the 'model diet' that should be followed;[3] looking at the diet given to the inmates of Berkhamsted Workhouse in 1836, two years after the New Poor Law came into effect, it is clear that bread and broth formed the basis of the diet.[4] Breakfast was bread and gruel, and there was little variety in the daily diet. Inmates would have struggled to get all the nutrients and calories they needed – and if they were put on the punishment diet, which was usually just bread and water – for any length of time, they would have rapidly weakened in strength.

Punishments given for such recalcitrance reflected a lack of understanding about what motivated these acts, and arguably failed to 'reform' miscreants. For example, at the Cirencester Workhouse in the last quarter of the nineteenth century, a first punishment for a woman who had committed a petty crime was to put her on a bread and water diet for twenty-four hours. If she committed another crime, then she would either be given another twenty-four hours on the diet, or forty-eight hours. Only after several offences would she be taken to the police and put before the courts. And even in court, there would only be a few limited options: she would either be discharged, given a caution, or a short prison sentence – of perhaps a week – and then returned to the workhouse. Those who immediately began rebelling on their return would then go on the diet again.

Men were more likely to face the Justices of the Peace for a first offence than women; boys would receive a flogging (such as that received by eleven-year-old George Weaving and ten-year-old John Bridges in 1884 after they 'dirtied' and 'damaged' their workhouse clothes[5]); girls might be locked in their dormitory (as the Moreman sisters were in January 1884; Louisa (fourteen), Julia (twelve), and Susan (ten), were punished for the afternoon after quarrelling with the woman in charge of their workhouse ward[6]). Laws were put in place to ensure that women couldn't be subject to corporal punishment, and that nursing mothers wouldn't be subject to the same discipline that others faced.[7]

The workhouse staff knew some families to be troublemakers. The Moremans, for example, were frequently in trouble; mainly Louisa, but also their mother Ellen. Young George Weaving was frequently being punished; in 1883, aged ten, he had tried to escape from the workhouse by climbing

Chipping Norton Workhouse.

over the external wall at 4.30 one morning. He had a few hours of freedom before being found by a policeman at 11.30 a.m. and promptly returned to the workhouse. He was locked up for the rest of the day, fed only bread and water for two days, and flogged. Given that he damaged his clothing shortly afterwards, it is arguable whether the flogging had much impact on his behaviour.[8]

Perhaps the most notorious family in Cirencester Workhouse during this time was the Glastonburys. Hannah Glastonbury was an inmate of the workhouse at the time of the 1871 census, when she was eighteen. She was a labourer's daughter from Siddington, who, when she worked, was a charwoman. Daniel Glastonbury, probably her grandfather, a seventy-five-year-old widower, was also an inmate at the same time, although her parents – Job and Sarah – were managing to keep themselves out of the workhouse, living and working in Siddington.

In 1877, Rosa Elizabeth Glastonbury was born in Cirencester – an illegitimate daughter of Hannah's.

By 1881, Hannah was in the workhouse with her four-year-old daughter, and she was still there two years later – although she had presumably had spells outside its environs in-between. On 12 February 1883, Hannah was punished by the workhouse master after quarrelling with other inmates, and given twenty-four hours on the bread-and-water diet.

Siddington, once home
to Hannah Glastonbury.

A month later, she refused to go into the dining hall when the bell rang for lunch, and was put on the meagre diet for another day. In May 1884, Hannah was punished with a day on bread and water for 'entering [a] yard appropriated to another class, and making a disturbance' and in August the same year was, along with six other women, given bread and water for 'disobedience to orders by going into infectious ward when occupied by a patient suffering from a contagious disease'. Four years later, and Hannah was still causing disturbances in the workhouse; in February 1888, she was taken before the magistrate after refusing to obey orders and breaking a window – however, she was discharged 'on promising to behave better'.

A year later, in September 1889, it was Hannah's daughter Rosa, then aged twelve, who was causing problems. She was alleged to have been repeatedly disobedient, threatened to smash a window, threatened to kill the woman in charge of her ward, and then tried to bite the schoolmistress. She was kept in bed for the day, and given bread and water. This was just the first in nearly fifty punishments that Rosa would receive over the next twenty or so years. She was in and out of the workhouse – in 1891, she was in Alverstoke, Hampshire, staying with church workers (perhaps an attempt by friends, family or acquaintances to improve her behaviour), but she seems to have been mainly in the workhouse, although never accepting of it.

Pages of the Workhouse Punishment Book are devoted to Rosa, whose crimes included swearing, violent behaviour, smashing of windows, fighting, insubordination and arson. Her punishments included frequent spells of bread and water diets, solitary confinement, time in prison, and a spell in a reformatory. Nothing worked. Between 1892 and 1893, she yo-yo'd between prison and the workhouse; as soon as she finished one prison sentence and returned to Cirencester Workhouse, she would be violent and be sent straight back before the magistrates.

There seems to have been no attempt to get her to work, or to try a different punishment on her, despite the evidence that prison held no fear for her. It says something that her most serious punishment – six weeks in prison – was given for burning the oakum she had been given to unpick, in September 1894. Refusing to do the mind-numbing work of the workhouse was seen as a more serious offence than trying to kill the staff or the other inmates (she received only three weeks in prison in 1899 for throwing boiling water over the workhouse nurse).

At some stage, Rosa became pregnant, giving birth to a child listed as Victoria Glastonbury in 1899 or 1900. Both were listed as residents of the workhouse in 1901. Shortly afterwards, Rosa married a fellow inmate – Nottingham coachbuilder Charles Dilks, a widower some thirty years her senior. By the winter of that year, the newlywed was still an inmate, receiving a police caution after ringing her dormitory bells for five hours one night before trying to hammer down the workhouse master's door.

In 1902, Rosa gave birth to her first legitimate child, a son named Victor (this seems to have been a different child to the earlier Victoria, despite the similarity in name, although Victoria then vanishes from the record). But in 1905, she was caught after absconding from the workhouse with Victor in her arms, and given another police caution. In 1909, now with two more children, she was charged with 'getting out of ward window and creating a great disturbance in the infirmary yard ringing the nurses' bell. Persistently going into the laundry and washhouses. Acting indecently (only partly dressed). Assaulting the Assistant Matron.' She was confined in the Refractory Cell between 12 p.m. and 9.20 p.m. between 15 and 17 July 1909, and on 19 July was sent to prison for three weeks.[9]

There are no more entries for Rosa between 1910 and when the punishment book ends in 1913. She lost one of her sons at the age of two in 1912, and another in 1920, when he was fifteen. Her husband died in 1912; but Rosa, ever persevering, married again in 1917, to Samuel Heath. Perhaps, in middle age she finally lost the urge to create mayhem and rebel against authority. Her multiple offences whilst supposedly being punished for simply being poor clearly show a lack of ability by the Poor Law Board of Guardians to adequately punish or rehabilitate such inmates.

Although there was a 'refractory cell' at Cirencester, it doesn't appear to have been used very much, with the bread and water diet being the preferred punishment, and usually deemed to be a sufficient punishment on its own.

However, Northleach Workhouse, although it punished inmates less frequently compared to Cirencester (which was, after all, a larger place with more inmates), used solitary confinement in a cell more often. The cell was windowless, and referred to as either the 'dark cell' or the 'punishment cell'.

The first person recorded in the Northleach Workhouse Punishment Book is Esther Johnson, who was found 'indecently exposing her person and using obscene language towards the inmates' on 17 January 1851.[10] She was locked in the dark cell for seven hours. The local Guardians have added a comment in the book – 'deservedly punished'.

Absconding from Northleach Workhouse usually resulted in inmates being sent before the magistrates and given short sentences to be served at Northleach House of Correction. However, some were given the bread and water diet – also referred to as a 'low', 'punishment' or 'gruel' diet - instead. There seemed little mathematics to this – it depended on how the staff felt as to how the matter was dealt with. So, while Harriet Potter was sent to the dark cell for four hours in 1851 for using abusive language,[11] Patience Scott, who was found guilty of the same offence in 1853, was taken before the local JP and sentenced to three weeks' hard labour at Northleach House of Correction.[12]

The diet in workhouses was neither large nor varied at the best of times. One wonders what the effect of giving inmates such a meagre diet was on their health. After being given bread and water to live on – and sometimes no daylight either, if they were also put in the dark cell – they were then returned to their usual diet, which wouldn't have been much more filling or nutritious. In the 1840s, there were severe concerns about the conditions in local prisons, after several prisoners at Northleach House of Correction became ill or died due to damp conditions and poor diet; but the workhouses weren't much better. Punishing poverty-stricken inmates with a lack of food and light would have affected them both physically and mentally.

Although there are only a couple of surviving Workhouse Punishment Books in Gloucester Archives, the Calendar of Prisoners for Gloucester Prison is full of accounts of workhouse inmates being punished with hard labour in the prison for deemed insubordination, and other poverty-related 'crimes'. Among the most common were either refusing to work, getting drunk, or absconding from the workhouse.

James Hall, for example, was jailed in 1885 for refusing to work in the workhouse. James, a fifty-year-old illiterate labourer who was in the Cirencester Workhouse, had, according to the workhouse records, been heard using profane language whilst staying on the casual ward,[13] had subsequently refused to work and was punished with ten days hard labour.

Later the same year, thirty-three-year-old shoemaker Robert Wilcox, originally from London, and also in the Cirencester Workhouse, was given the same sentence for refusing to work. John Grainger (twenty-five) and John Brookes (twenty-one) were labourers who were given fourteen days' hard labour in 1886 for refusing to work in the same workhouse, as was Charles Shurmes, a forty-six-year-old gardener.[14]

Tetbury Workhouse.

Northleach Workhouse.

Although the Cirencester Workhouse seems to have had more than its fair share of problems, other workhouses struggled to deal with their inmates, too. Thirty-one-year-old Joseph Thompson was given fourteen days' imprisonment for absconding from the Stow-on-the-Wold Workhouse in 1886 and in the same year, Tetbury Workhouse inmate Richard Bennett (forty-eight), received a sentence of ten days after absconding.[15] Local policemen often picked up the inmates who had absconded within a few hours; occasionally, family members would report their own relatives for absconding, reluctant to pay to maintain them and preferring the parish to do so.

Charles Watts was a frequent absconder from Northleach Workhouse, and caused policemen from all over the Cotswolds work. In May 1898, aged fifty-two, he absconded and was arrested by the police at Bourton-on-the-Water, receiving a fourteen-day prison sentence. In 1902, he ran away and was found by police at Little Barrington four days later. On this occasion, he received a police caution 'on account of his mental condition'.

A year later, he was again discovered by police at Little Barrington wearing workhouse clothes, three days after absconding from Northleach, and was

Bourton-on-the-Water, where Charles Watts was found in 1898.

Little Barrington, where Charles absconded in 1899.

again cautioned; three weeks later, he was caught closer to home, trying to climb over the wall of the men's yard at the workhouse, and given four hours in the workhouse's dark cell and two meals of bread and water as a punishment. In 1904, he was given fourteen days' hard labour after being found at Woodstock; in 1907, he was caught near Stow-on-the-Wold after absconding from the workhouse on Christmas Day. He had five days of freedom before being found and given fourteen days' hard labour.[16]

One has to admire Charles' perseverance and fitness – spending some nine years, on and off, escaping and managing to evade arrest for several days at a time. One man wasn't as lucky as this serial absconder; fifty-six-year-old George Stephens was given fourteen days' hard labour in March 1885 after absconding from the Stow Workhouse. He was taken to prison, and died there two days later.[17]

Some inmates went to great lengths to abscond, such as twenty-three-year-old Elizabeth Parker, who, in October 1910, escaped Northleach Workhouse by crawling through a window and clambering down the walls. Unfortunately for her, she was found by police at Eastington and promptly returned to the workhouse, where she was given two meals on the punishment diet. A month later, she was caught trying to escape via the same window and given another two meals of bread and water.[18]

The punishments recorded for inmates who repeatedly offended show how the workhouses failed to control such behaviour through their limited punishments. The multiple entries for William Harris, an inmate in his mid-sixties, illustrate this. He was frequently caught trying to abscond from Northleach Workhouse between 1909 and 1910, usually by climbing over the boundary wall. In 1909, he was caught trying to escape on 15 December, 16 December, 17 December, 21 December and 24 December, and on each occasion put in the dark cell for four hours, and fed only bread and water for four meals. Four days later, he was put in the cell for three hours and given two meals of 'low diet'. On 26 March 1910, he received five hours in the dark cell and one meal of bread and water; a day later, he was put in prison for a day; on 2 April and 4 April, he was put in the dark cell for five hours per day and given one meal of bread and water; on 11 April, six hours in the cell and one meal of bread and water; 24 April and 28 April two hours each day in the cell; and finally, on 1 May 1910, he was given a fourteen-day prison sentence.[19] One senses almost a desperation amongst the authorities about what to do with such errant inmates; locking them in a dark cell on their own almost amounted to 'out of sight, out of mind', at least for a few hours.

Gloucester Street, Winchcombe, where the town's workhouse was located.

A common action by workhouse inmates was to destroy their own clothes, to prevent them being discharged by the workhouse; to make the Poor Law Union have to expend more money in reclothing them; or simply to make their grievances known. Grantley Rose, a sixty-seven-year-old miner originally from Taunton, was given ten days' hard labour for destroying his own clothes in Cirencester Workhouse; twenty-seven-year-old James Thomas and Frank Wright, twenty-eight, were both given fourteen days' hard labour for destroying their clothes in the Stow Workhouse in 1885. A year later, in the Winchcombe Workhouse, twenty-five-year-old Scottish labourer Thomas Wilson was given fourteen days for the same offence.[20]

Others were penalised for trying to obtain money, or shelter. Francis Smith, sixty-three, was sentenced to fourteen days' hard labour in Cirencester in August 1885, for 'gathering alms under false pretences'. Twenty-three-year-old Daniel Andrews was arrested in Withington for trying to sleep in a brickyard and was given ten days' hard labour; William Smith was more unlucky; when he tried to sleep in the same or a nearby brickyard in Withington, he received fourteen days. Sixty-two-year-old John Spencer was arrested for begging in Cirencester in 1884 and given fourteen days' hard labour.[21]

John Otsao, a South American sailor, was convicted of applying for workhouse relief 'whilst in possession of £1½d' in January 1885 and given fourteen days' hard labour. It seems a bit harsh; Otsao, who was said to have the aliases of Ottast, O'Tassa and Otasso (more an issue with the authorities misspelling or mispronouncing his South American name), was a fifty-six-year-old man with no schooling bar his education on the seas. He had ended up in a strange part of the world, and was trying to preserve the savings he had. But you had to be completely destitute to merit any kind of help, and so he was punished. Presumably, his savings were taken or spent, for two months later, after serving his initial sentence, Otsao was again in prison, this time serving seven days' hard labour for begging.[22]

There were acts of kindness to those in the workhouse, on occasion; such as the gift of twenty hares sent by the Earl of Eldon to the inmates of Northleach Workhouse in 1873, to celebrate the earl's success at hare-shooting over his estates at Chedworth and Stowell.[23] Gifts from Guardians or wealthy locals were often common at Christmas time, enabling the inmates to have a Christmas dinner that was marginally more interesting than their usual fare.

But for every charitable act, there was a petty crime and an illogical punishment. The workhouse could be a punishment in itself. In 1843, the *Bristol Mercury* noted the death of a man it referred to as 'a veteran pauper'. Eighty-five-year-old Richard Williams had died on 14 December 1843 at the Cirencester Union Workhouse. The newspaper noted, 'He was admitted into the old workhouse upwards of seventy years ago, in consequence of an injury sustained in falling from a window in the Yellow School, when a boy in that institution; he has never slept out of the Cirencester Workhouse for the time above stated'.[24] So poor Richard was admitted to the workhouse at the age of fifteen, injured; and wasn't able to leave it until he died, seventy years later.

Workhouse inmates often fought each other, or stole from their fellow inmates, despite each having few possessions. In 1883, Henry Merchant, a 'well known' inhabitant of the Cirencester Workhouse, stole a pocket knife from fellow inmate William Midwinter. The case was heard at the petty session in Cirencester, where the local police superintendent said that 'the prisoner was a very bad character and spent all his time either in gaol or in the workhouse. He had been sent to penal servitude for stealing a knife, and was at present under police supervision.'[25] Merchant was sent again from workhouse to prison for this offence, serving three months' hard labour.

Likewise, David Woodcock, an inmate in the Witney Workhouse just over the border into West Oxfordshire, was given three weeks' hard labour in 1849 for 'having misconducted himself in the Union House'.[26]

The workhouse masters were always at pains to publicise the merits of their workhouses, and disliked criticism. However, the national media could be less than kind about their efforts. In 1867, the *Pall Mall Gazette* had a bit of a snigger at the master of the Stow-on-the-Wold Workhouse, following a complaint made to it by one resident, Henry Maiden (going under the pseudonym of 'Tramp'), that its bedding, which he called a rug, was full of vermin. The master responded by saying that inmates were given blankets, not rugs, and that there were no vermin in the workhouse – just fleas. *The Pall Mall Gazette* responded, 'it is notable from this correspondence that, in workhouse parlance, rugs are not blankets, and fleas are not vermin'.[27]

One could argue that finding fleas – at the very least – in one's bedding was in itself a punishment for being put in the workhouse. But the Consolidated General Order issued to workhouses in 1847 made a comprehensive list of punishments that miscreant paupers could expect to receive.

Minor offences listed in the Consolidated Order included the making of noise when inmates had been told to be quiet, playing at cards, feigning illness, failing to wash properly, and misbehaving during prayers. Being found to have done any of these things would classify the inmate as 'disorderly'. One level up from this was drunkenness, causing damage to workhouse property (which included the workhouse clothes inmates were forced to wear), and acting indecently or writing obscene things. These offences would be classified as 'refractory'.

Article 129 of the Consolidated Order gave the workhouse master permission to punish a pauper classified as disorderly by giving him or her a maximum of forty-eight hours on the punishment diet and withdrawing the usual allowances of butter, cheese, tea, sugar or broth. A refractory inmate could be punished with this diet, and also by solitary confinement, but for no longer than twenty-four hours. However, if this was deemed insufficient, the master could send the inmate to a Justice of the Peace, who could allow further confinement if necessary.

Anyone over the age of twelve could be subject to solitary confinement and boys under the age of fourteen could be flogged as long as the punishment was carried out by either the schoolmaster or the workhouse master – and both should, ideally, be present for the flogging. Those who were punished with solitary confinement between 8 p.m. and 6 a.m. had to be provided with a bed and bedding. The sick, pregnant and nursing mothers, as well as those either under twelve or over sixty, were not allowed to be given the punishment diet or confinement.[28]

However, there was one codicil. If the Medical Officer wrote specifying that an inmate's health wouldn't be affected by the punishment, these classes of inmate could be punished in that way, so these exemptions weren't as liberal as it appears. The offences of bringing drink into the workhouse, or trying to abscond from it, were supposed to be punished by taking the miscreant before the Justice of the Peace to be dealt with – although in the Cotswolds, the master often tried to deal with initial offences with internal punishments first.

Article 140 of the General Order specified that no corporal punishment should be carried out on a boy until at least two hours had passed since he had committed the crime. In Worcestershire in 1848, one workhouse school master was dismissed when it was found he had failed to obey this rule. Henry Charles Ellins, of Kidderminster Poor Law Union Workhouse, had 'improperly punished a boy under his charge' because he was 'unaware of the provisions of Article 140'.[29] It was hardly surprising that he didn't know the numerous rules and regulations off by heart.

What is clear is that workhouse life was strictly regimented, and any attempts to do things differently were strictly punished. But the punishments laid down were limited, and predictable, and took little account of how much some inhabitants disliked the workhouse regime, and how desperate they were to avoid it.

## Notes

1 *Morning Chronicle*, 15 September 1848
2 *The Times*, 27 November 1837, p. 5
3 Trevor May (1997), p. 22
4 Trevor May (1997), p. 23
5 Cirencester Workhouse Punishment Book, entry for 10 January 1884, Gloucestershire Archives reference G/CI/87
6 Cirencester Workhouse Punishment Book, entry for 13 January 1884, Gloucestershire Archives reference G/CI/87
7 Simon Fowler (2007), p. 117
8 Cirencester Workhouse Punishment Book, entry for 10 July 1883, Gloucestershire Archives reference G/CI/87

[9] Cirencester Workhouse Punishment Book, various entries between 12 February 1883 and 19 July 1909, Gloucestershire Archives reference G/CI/87

[10] Northleach Workhouse Punishment Book, entry for 17 January 1851, Gloucestershire Archives reference G/NO/87

[11] Northleach Workhouse Punishment Book, entry for 18 February 1851, Gloucestershire Archives reference G/NO/87

[12] Northleach Workhouse Punishment Book, entry for 3 November 1853, Gloucestershire Archives reference G/NO/87

[13] Cirencester Workhouse Punishment Book, entry for 19 February 1885, Gloucestershire Archives reference G/CI/87

[14] Calendar of Prisoners, Gloucestershire Archives reference Q/SG2/1885-6

[15] Calendar of Prisoners, Gloucestershire Archives reference Q/SG2/1886

[16] Northleach Workhouse Punishment Book, various entries between 24 May 1898 and 25 December 1907, Gloucestershire Archives reference G/NO/87

[17] Calendar of Prisoners, Gloucestershire Archives reference Q/SG2/1885

[18] Northleach Workhouse Punishment Book, entries for 23 October 1910 and 13 November 1910, Gloucestershire Archives reference G/NO/87

[19] Northleach Workhouse Punishment Book, various entries between 15 December 1909 and 1 May 1910, Gloucestershire Archives reference G/NO/87

[20] Calendar of Prisoners, Gloucestershire Archives reference Q/SG/1885-6

[21] Calendar of Prisoners, Gloucestershire Archives reference Q/SG/1884-5

[22] Calendar of Prisoners, Gloucestershire Archives reference Q/SG/1885

[23] *Jackson's Oxford Journal*, 17 January 1874

[24] *Bristol Mercury*, 30 December 1843

[25] *Bristol Mercury*, 4 December 1883

[26] *Oxford Journal*, 3 November 1849

[27] *Pall Mall Gazette*, 1 August 1867

[28] Transcript of the 1847 General Consolidated Order by Peter Higginbotham, on his website http://www.workhouses.org.uk/index.html?gco/gco1847intro.shtml

[29] National Archives reference MH12/14019

# 11

# SCHOOL PUNISHMENTS

Throughout the nineteenth century, floggings, canings and beatings were the norm at schools throughout the Cotswolds, as corporal punishment was viewed as a vital way of promoting good behaviour in errant boys.

In 1825, an anonymous reporter for the *New Monthly Magazine*[1] was referring to the violence of school punishments at the end of the eighteenth century as something from the distant past, saying the 'cruel fondness' of headmasters for punishing children had been replaced by 'smiles and flowers'. He had written about a 'Master of the Old School' who had 'little cruel eyes' and, despite being a clergyman, would flog his students with 'wrath', shouting, 'Gad's my life!' and lecturing the children in between blows. The reporter points out, 'I could tell tales of this man's cruelty and unjustice almost inconceivable in many such school as we have at present'.

Yet this author may have been living in a different world, for such cruelty was still inflicted on children throughout the nineteenth century, despite changes and improvements in the education system. Although attention was increasingly brought to bear on cases that were seen to be abnormally violent, courts were reluctant to punish headmasters, as they were viewed as respectable members of society who were merely trying to get children to behave.

In 1843, a scandal threatened to envelop the genteel town of Winchcombe, after the master of the Winchcombe Free School, Charles Lapworth, was accused of cruelty towards one of his pupils. The pupil, Conrad Algernon Carter, was alleged to have been beaten by the master, to the extent that he had died of his injuries.

At the end of January 1844, an inquiry was held into the master's behaviour, after a coroner had called his conduct into question. The inquiry, which took three days, was held at the Town Hall in Winchcombe, where the coroner's jury was charged with deciding what had happened at the school.

Lord Sudeley, from Sudeley Castle, a descendant of the school's founder, John Brown of Salperton, and the Revd Reginald Wynniat of Guiting Grange were the school trustees in charge of the inquiry, which saw crowds attending each of its three days. Attendees included magistrates, clergy and local gentry, as well as other trustees – the Honourable Charles Hanbury Tract, and Winchcombe vicar John Harvey.

Sudeley Castle, home of school trustee Lord Sudeley.

Conrad was from a good family, being the youngest son of local solicitor Giles Carter. Aged twelve, Conrad was viewed as a promising youth, who had attended the grammar school since he was nine. He was a healthy, spirited boy, but in March 1843 he had been severely punished by Mr Lapworth for what was seen as a 'very slight transgression'.[2]

The trustees, headed by Lord Sudeley, wanted to see whether it was correct, as reported by *The Times*, that Conrad Carter had been the victim of corporal punishment that had overstepped the boundaries of what was acceptable. The newspapers had been of the opinion that he had been 'violently and unmercifully beaten' with a cane in a manner that 'discredited' the school master.[3]

Allegedly, he had initially been caned until he had fallen over. Conrad threatened to run away from school and tell his father what Lapworth had done; and as a result, Lapworth continued beating him, but more severely.

Conrad had fainted from the beating he had been given. When he came round, his friends asked him to show where he had been beaten; he took off his shirt, and showed red, green and black neck and arms, with a swollen shoulder.

Conrad was taken out of school and looked after at home from then on. He was bed-bound, and continuously unwell until September, suffering from sores and ulcers. He then declined rapidly and died on 31 December 1843.

Although it was concluded that Conrad Carter had actually died from ulceration of the lungs, the coroner's jury had been unable to decide whether the ulceration was caused by the earlier beating, or whether the actions of Mr Lapworth had exacerbated a previous condition.

There certainly seemed to have been animosity between Carter and his master. The latter had ordered the other schoolboys not to associate with Carter during school hours – an action that the original coroner's jury had found to be 'cruel'[4].

But the trustees rejected much of the coroner's jury's findings. The initial findings, upheld by the coroner, had been that Carter had been bruised and ulcerated on the head, neck, arms and shoulders, and that these injuries caused his premature death.

However, by the time Lord Sudeley had investigated, the trustees decided the boy had simply fallen over, rather than dying from a beating. The trustees then decided that Carter had been to blame for his woes, because he had previously been 'insubordinate' on more than one occasion. They also decided that Mr Lapworth, the headmaster, had suffered because of

Trustee Revd Wynniat lived here at Guiting Grange.

Another trustee, John Harvey, was vicar of St Peter's, Winchcombe.

the stigma that had resulted from the pupil's death, and that was sufficient 'punishment' for him – even though they had earlier stated that he had done nothing to warrant 'punishing'!

Conrad's father, Giles, failed in his attempt to bring a charge of unjustifiable and cruel assault against Lapworth; he was persuaded by the trustees to withdraw the charge, with Lapworth paying the expenses he had occurred, which amounted to twenty shillings.[5]

The trustees had been anxious to preserve the image of the school and its teachers. Reverend John Harvey, one of these trustees, had previously written to *The Times*, after it published a scathing report of Conrad's treatment, slating the dead child for his 'insubordination'.

Harvey proudly stated that, after being told Conrad had received a flogging, he said, 'If my child had misconducted himself at school as Conrad had, I should expect that he would receive the same or worse.' He then went on to blame Giles Carter for his son's death, implying that it was his fault for moving his family to Cleeve Hill, 'in a very bleak and exposed situation'. Mr Harvey claimed that it was this move that led to Conrad's mother dying of a 'bad cold' in November 1843, and must also have been the cause of Conrad becoming consumptive.[6]

It was clearly in the trustees' interests to uphold the reputation both of the school and of themselves. If they had to smear the name of both a local solicitor and his twelve-year-old deceased son, then that is what they would do.

After this mockery of a court hearing, Charles Lapworth was able to keep his job, and Conrad Carter's sufferings were forgotten. Those who had written to the papers after the coroner's inquest to express their upset at Conrad's treatment were either convinced by the trustees' account, or realised that the matter was now, officially, closed.

Nine years later, in December 1853, another case was heard not far from Winchcombe. Cheltenham County Court heard a case where thirteen-year-old George John Mickenright sued Andrew Livingstone, Drill-Sergeant at Cheltenham Grammar School, and headmaster Dr Humphreys, after he was flogged twice by Livingstone, under the direction of Humphreys. The first flogging was twelve lashes of a riding whip, as punishment for Mickenright arguing with some of the boys at the rival Cheltenham College. He was then given another twelve lashes after throwing a cracker in the fire. Mickenright rebelled against the punishments, refusing to take his coat off when asked, and kicking Livingstone. Dr Humphreys then ordered eighteen lashes as an additional punishment.

After the whipping, Mickenright's back, from neck to waist, was described as having 'the appearance of newly cut meat, with a thin skin over it. It was in a dreadful state'. Another boy, who had received twelve lashes at the same time, gave evidence saying that he had had a fit as a result of his own punishment.

The defence argued that 'whipping was only a reasonable and moderate chastisement', with a witness, arguing that Livingstone was 'universally beloved by the boys' and that Dr Humphreys was 'averse to flogging, and that there was much less corporal punishment in the school than usual'. Unusually, however, the judge found in favour of George Mickenright, and granted him four guineas in damages.[7]

The issue continued to be debated in the newspapers, with cases from around England being reported in the media. In 1875, it was noted that one of the masters of Stafford Grammar School had been fined ten shillings and costs after caning a schoolboy for 'smiling'.[8] Five years later, Thomas Bullock, head of a national school in Westminster, was charged with assault on eight-year-old Frederick Teasdale after Bullock boxed his ears and gave him a black eye. Teasdale's crime was being unable to answer some questions during a Scripture lesson. The school had a punishment regime that involved caning the hand and boxing ears. It was found that the punishment was 'reprehensible', and that boxing ears was 'improper', and the head was fined 40 shillings and costs.[9]

In 1888, Mr Atkinson, head of the Morecambe School for Boys in Lancashire, had to explain himself to a school board enquiry, after caning a child for not doing his spellings correctly (the child in question had got one spelling out of the ten set wrong). It was argued, by a defender of Atkinson, that 'if they took away the right to punish from the headmaster, they took away all authority.' Interestingly, in this case, the chairman of the enquiry stated that he believed 'there was less corporal punishment in proportion to the teacher's ability'. Although Atkinson was not punished, a change was made to the school's administration, with all instances of corporal punishment having to be recorded in detail.[10]

These cases involved both male and female teachers. In Guernsey in 1895, a Miss Bowman, headmistress of the St Peter Port Ragged School, was charged with caning a Miss Terry. However, she stated that the child was 'unmanageable', and the father – who had initially reported Miss Bowman to the local constable – decided not to press charges.[11]

The education system was changing during this time, with the passing of such legislation as the Elementary Education Act of 1870, designed to give all children schooling between the ages of five and twelve. The Act brought in Board Schools – regulated by school boards in the Poor Law Unions – to run alongside Church schools. But the complaints continued, and the debate over when corporal punishment could be deemed to have gone too far was still alive in 1900, when a case was heard at the Chadlington Petty Sessions in West Oxfordshire. John Hopson, the head of the Charlbury Board School, had been summoned on the charge of committing an assault on the son of one Henry Harrison, whilst the child was at school on 12 November.

Henry Harrison, a widower who worked as a commercial traveller and hairdresser, said that his nine-year-old son, Raymond, had arrived home from school at 4.45 p.m. with a large wheal on his forehead. There were also wounds to his legs and hands, with blood still running out of them. The child was shocked and nervous, and had to be put to bed.

Harrison said that he was opposed to corporal punishment, but hadn't raised his objections with the school, as he didn't want to interfere with how they disciplined their pupils. He had, though, raised the issue after seeing his son's injuries, and remarked that Mr Jones, a member of the school board with whom he had talked, 'appeared to be so disinterested' and had said the wheals were 'such a trivial matter not to be worth talking about'.

The emphasis at the Petty Sessions seemed to be to destroy the reputation of Harrison, rather than question the respectable Mr Hopson too much. It was alleged that when the family had previously lived in Witney, Mr Harrison's children had been known to be troublesome and Raymond was 'sullen'. The NSPCC had been called out to Henry Harrison's home but 'were not able to bring a charge against him'.

It could be that the Harrisons had struggled to discipline their large family. Henry and his wife Georgina had had six surviving children – Frank Reginald George, Elsie, Raymond, Gordon, Linda and Evelyn, born between 1887 and 1896. Life must have been even more difficult after Georgina's death, at the age of forty-one, in 1898, which left Henry struggling to manage work and childcare.

Chipping Norton police station, where the Chadlington Petty Sessions, which covered Charlbury, were held.

Broadwell, home to Henry Betteridge and Reginald Goddard.

When Mr Harrison took his son to the doctor, he was, he said, 'ridiculed', with the doctor saying that 'he had been served much worse at school himself'.

Amelia Harrison – Henry's unmarried sister, with whom he and his children lived - gave evidence, and said there had been 'a great deal of bother lately at Charlbury about corporal punishment; she did not believe in whipping children.' She was accused of bringing the case not out of concern for her nephew, but as a means of advancing the 'theoretical controversy about the right of punishment in school at Charlbury'. She understandably refuted this.

It seems that Charlbury residents had been giving the school board a lot of difficulty about the use of corporal punishment at school. They were against it; the board saw it as a fundamental part of maintaining discipline. The petty sessions heard, from the defence, that nobody denied that young Harrison had been punished by the head, and this was the cause of his injuries. However, it was argued that 'a great mountain had been made out of a little matter', and that the punishment was necessary because of the boy's sullenness, and not made out of a personal vindictiveness of the head towards this particular pupil.

The case was dismissed, and Mr Hopson told he would leave the court 'without the slightest stain upon his character'.[12]

Some cases were heard where children had committed crimes at their school, although outside of the normal school day. Also in 1900, a case was heard at the Stow-on-the-Wold Petty Sessions against two boys in the nearby village of Broadwell.

The boys were Henry Betteridge, eight, who lived with his widowed mother Elizabeth and older brother William (at sixteen, the only income earner in the family), and Reginald Goddard, ten, who also lived in the village with a widowed mother, with an older brother and sister. They were accused of breaking into the Broadwell school while the headmaster was absent, 'playing havoc with the books, pens, pencils, crayons, etc, and also for breaking open a missionary box'.[13]

One could argue that the boys, growing up without a father (Reginald's father had died before his first birthday), with widowed mothers busy trying to keep the house going and older siblings labouring to earn money for the family, were seeking attention; or that they lacked respect for a school that they would soon be leaving, in order to get a labouring job themselves and earn more family income.

In court, though, nothing was heard of their family background, and the boys were ordered to be whipped as punishment.

Bibury: One resident was still arguing in favour of the cane in the 1950s.

In 1902, Balfour's Education Act abolished the 2,568 school boards and replaced them with local education authorities. These 300 authorities took over the supervision of nearly 6,000 board schools across England and Wales.

In 1952, a correspondent from Bibury wrote to *The Times* in support of 'that last-surviving instrument of torture, the cane'. The Cotswold resident said that judicious use of the cane would 'break down the obduracy with which young offenders are apt to confront authority. For a few minutes after he has been caned, he will be prepared to listen; and the value of the caning will depend upon what is said to him then – and above all upon who says it.'[14]

So the debate over the merits or otherwise of corporal punishment in schools rumbled on throughout the nineteenth and twentieth centuries. It was only made illegal in English state schools in 1987; private schools could continue to use such punishments until 1999. Until this point, children could still be punished with strikes from a cane, slipper, or leather strap.

# Notes

[1] Repeated in the *Examiner's* newspaper Chat column of 18 December 1825

[2] *Hampshire Advertiser*, 13 January 1844

[3] *Jackson's Oxford Journal*, 3 February 1844

[4] *Hampshire Advertiser*, 13 January 1844

[5] *Bristol Mercury*, 20 January 1844

[6] *The Times*, letters, 16 January 1844

[7] *Berrow's Worcester Journal*, Sat 17 December 1853, p. 3

[8] *The Graphic*, Sat 22 May, 1875

[9] *Morning Post*, 4 November 1880

[10] *Lancaster Gazette and General Advertiser for Lancashire, Westmorland and Yorkshire*, 6 October 1888

[11] *The Star*, St Peter Port, Tue 11 June 1895

[12] All quotes about the Harrison case are taken from *Jackson's Oxford Journal*, 1 December 1900

[13] *Jackson's Oxford Journal*, 8 September 1900

[14] *The Times*, 4 October 1952

# CONCLUSION

By 1800, it was clear that punishing offenders did not necessarily reduce the crime rate. The *Gloucester Journal* reported:

> We observe with concern a great increase in the number of prisoners that fill the calendar for the ensuing Assizes; they amount to no less than 46, and many of them are for capital offences.[1]

The issue of how to punish those convicted of offences has been the topic of conversation amongst politicians, media and the public for centuries. Should the emphasis be on punishment or on rehabilitation? If the former, then what punishment is most efficacious?

By the end of George IV's reign, enlightened members of the Cotswold community were beginning to publicly express their doubt in the success of capital punishment in deterring people from committing crimes. In particular, they wondered whether hanging men and women for petty crimes, such as fraud or forgery, was necessary or desirable.

In the spring of 1830, many towns across England organised petitions against the use of capital punishment for forgery cases. This was a reaction to Robert Peel's proposed amendments to the law, which argued that the death penalty as a punishment would be abolished – but only in cases where the sentence had been recorded, but not carried out. The petitioners argued that the sentence should never be recorded or carried out for crimes involving forgery.

The towns that petitioned Sir Robert Peel, the then Home Secretary, included larger cities such as Newcastle and York – but also the Cotswold towns of Chipping Norton and Cirencester, where 'Magistrates, Clergy, Bankers, and other respectable inhabitants' of the towns added their signatures, according to the *Oxford Journal*.[2]

By July 1832, the bill proposing the abolition of the death penalty for certain felonies had been passed. These felonies included the stealing of cattle or property to the amount of £5 in a dwelling house, 'to which species of crime the penalty of death attached by Acts of the 7th and 8th George IV, and the 9th George IV.' For these crimes, the new bill originally changed the punishment to transportation for life, or for seven years, or for a jail sentence of under four years. The more conservative House of Lords, though, removed the alternative sentences and insisted that convicted criminals should simply be transported for life.

However, as technology developed – resulting in the construction of faster and more efficient ships – the fear of transportation decreased. More became known about the convict colonies and life there, and some saw it as a new start, an escape from the troubles of their former lives. Transportation was no longer a deterrent to those seeking to commit crime.

Throughout the eighteenth and nineteenth centuries, juries had the power to convict the accused person – and they frequently showed a reluctance to find someone guilty of an offence where they might be condemned to death as a result. In such cases, they might instead find a person guilty of a lesser offence, thus getting round the country's sometimes draconian punishments. So a person originally accused of rape, for example, might instead be found guilty of the lesser charge of assault, and escape the death penalty.

The unfortunate flipside of this was that there was less incentive for women to give evidence in rape cases, knowing that juries would be less likely to convict of that offence, and that prosecutors would attempt to draw into question a woman's morality and earlier life, in order to blame her, and make it easier to acquit the accused.

In 1836, a petition was made to the House of Commons, signed by Gloucestershire magistrates, as well as by local residents. The petition stated that the system of criminal justice in England would be improved if lesser crimes were tried by magistrates locally, rather than by the assizes or quarter sessions. There were some interesting statistics quoted in the petition, such as the fact that in the previous year, 1835, there was a total of 372 convicts in Gloucestershire. One-hundred-and-four of those were sentenced to imprisonment for three months or less, 'with or without hard labour, solitary confinement, or whipping'. Fifty-five of these were sentenced to two months or less. Twenty out of the original one-hundred-and-four, and ten out of the fifty-five were under seventeen years of age when they were convicted.[3]

There was clearly a recognition that trying those accused of petty crimes at the quarter sessions involved a lot of resources, and it would be more efficient to try such people at a local level. At around this time, the use of the stocks was falling out of favour, with it being reserved for those who had been told to pay a fine after being convicted of an offence such as being drunk, and had failed to pay the money within the required period of time. Whipping was also decreasing in popularity, leaving prison or financial penalties as the punishment of choice for petty criminals.

Transportation also decreased in the Cotswolds during this time, with more of those sentenced to transportation in fact serving their sentences in the UK, either in prisons or on the notorious prison hulks. However, the death penalty remained in place, and it took far longer for calls for its abolition to be heard – although changes were made during the nineteenth century, such as the move from public hangings to private ones, within the confines the of prison walls.

Gloucester Prison still exists today. Built as the County Gaol in 1782, on the site of the old Gloucester Castle, it was rebuilt in 1840 and is now a Category B men's prison, with a young offenders' wing added in the 1980s. Although prison life has changed considerably since the eighteenth and nineteenth centuries, it is interesting to note that in 2007, the prison was criticised by the Independent Monitoring Board for overcrowding, poor dining provision and cramped cells[4] - the Victorian press reports into conditions at Northleach House of Correction come to mind.

Northleach House of Correction has seen a bigger change than Gloucester Prison. It is now a museum, café and site of the Cotswolds Discovery Centre, which aims to relate the history of the area to visitors. Although it looks a striking building, a glimpse at the old cells, some of which are now preserved and open to the public, still conjure up a dark vision of what life in the Cotswolds could be like.

## Notes

[1] *Gloucester Journal*, 10 March 1800
[2] *Jackson's Oxford Journal*, 10 April 1830
[3] *Jackson's Oxford Journal*, 13 February 1836
[4] 'Prison Conditions Are Criticised', BBC News, 20 June 2007, accessed via http://news.bbc.co.uk/1/hi/england/gloucestershire/6220888.stm

# BIBLIOGRAPHY

Darby, Nell, *Foul Deeds and Suspicious Deaths in the Cotswolds* (Pen & Sword, Barnsley, 2009)

Darvill, Timothy and Gerrard, Christopher, *Cirencester: Town and Landscape* (Alan Sutton, Stroud, 1994)

Donaldson, D.N., *Winchcombe: A History of the Cotswold Borough* (The Wychwood Press, Charlbury, 2001)

Fowler, Simon, *Workhouse* (National Archives, Kew, 2007)

Harrison, Ross, *Bentham* (Routledge, London, 1983)

Herbert, N.M. (ed.), *A History of the County of Gloucester: Volume 11* (OUP/ Institute for Historical Research, Oxford, 1976)

Herbert, N.M. (ed.), *A History of the County of Gloucester: Volume 4: The City of Gloucester* (OUP/Institute of Historical Research, 1988)

Hodgson, Eric, *A History of Tetbury* (Tetbury Civic Society/Alan Sutton, Dursley, 1976)

Johnson, Joan, *Stow on the Wold* (Alan Sutton, Stroud, 1994)

May, Trevor, *The Victorian Workhouse* (Shire, Princes Risborough, 1997)

Muir, Richard, *The Landscape Encyclopaedia* (Windgather Press, Macclesfield, 2004)

Taylor, David, *Crime, Policing and Punishment in England 1750-1914* (Palgrave Macmillan, Basingstoke, 1998)

Other titles published by The History Press

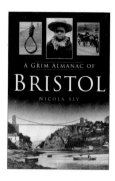

## A Grim Almanac of Bristol

NICOLA SLY

*A Grim Almanac of Bristol* is a day-by-day catalogue of 365 ghastly tales from the city's past. There are murders, manslaughters and bizarre deaths, such as the mother who mistakenly fed her child rat poison instead of teething powders, and the deaths of a man and his wife from a gas leak, both of which occurred in 1861. There is an assortment of disasters and devastating fires, not to mention mining disasters, rail crashes, explosions, shipwrecks, cases of cruelty and neglect and a plethora of uncanny accidents. Generously illustrated, this chronicle is an entertaining and readable record of Bristol's grim past. Read on ... if you dare!

978 0 7524 5934 9

## A Grim Almanac of Gloucestershire

ROBIN BROOKS

This compilation of macabre misery, wanton wickedness and murky misfortune reminds us that sometimes Lady Fate doesn't simply point her fickle finger at an unfortunate soul — she jabs them full in the eye. Gloucestershire is especially good at blending the quaint with the brutal. There is much between these covers that will make you raise an eyebrow, curl a toe and cross your legs. Prepare for your stomach to be turned, your brow to be furrowed and your funny bones to be tickled by these true tales of Grim Gloucestershire.

978 0 7524 5679 9

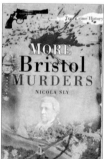

## More Bristol Murders

NICOLA SLY

This chilling follow-up to *Bristol Murders* brings together more true-life historical murders that shocked not only the city but made headline news throughout the nation. They include the brutal murder of policemen Patrick White and Christopher Wickham in 1862, a frightful case of murder and suicide at Bitton in 1842, and the deliberate starvation of a child at Bedminster in 1874. Also included are several twentieth century cases, among them the 1942 killing of Lilian Austin in Redlands, the 1951 murder of Peggy Lye, and the still unsolved murder of Louise Dunne at Easton in 1967.

978 0 7524 5617 1

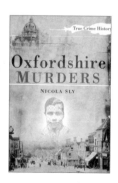

## Oxfordshire Murders

NICOLA SLY

*Oxfordshire Murders* brings together twenty-five murderous tales, some which were little known outside the county, and others which made national headlines. Contained within the pages of this book are the stories behind some of the most heinous crimes ever committed in Oxfordshire. They include the deaths of two gamekeepers, brutally murdered in 1824 and 1835; Henrietta Walker, killed by her husband at Chipping Norton in 1887; Mary Allen, shot by Harry Rowles at Cassington in the same year; and Anne Kempson, murdered by Henry Seymour, a door-to-door salesman, in Oxford in 1931.

978 0 7524 5359 0

Visit our website and discover thousands of other History Press books.

**www.thehistorypress.co.uk**